THE OEDIPUS PLAYS

OEDIPUS THE KING
OEDIPUS AT COLONUS

Sophocles

in new versions by
Ranjit Bolt

REGENT'S
UNIVERSITY LONDON

a b s o l u t e   c l a s s i c s

First published in 1996 by Absolute Classics, an imprint of
Absolute Press, Scarborough House, 29 James Street West,
Bath BA1 2BT, England

Cover and text design: Ian Middleton

Printed by the Longdunn Press Ltd, Bristol.

ISBN 1 899791 95 7

FOREWORD

I've always taken a more or less gloomy view of life myself (at least, it *seems* like always now) and perhaps that's why I felt such a strong sense of identification with these plays. If the translations work, it may well have something to do with the fact that the chorus's reflection in the second play: "Never to have been born is best by far." seems to me to be patently obvious. I dare say it does to many, at any rate some of the time, and therein lies the power of Sophocles' dark "take" on the human condition. It is given an equally gloomy formulation in the first play: "No man is truly happy, none; we only dream we're happy; then, almost at once the dream is gone." All right, Sophocles is saying, Oedipus may have had it worst – the worst ever – but we all have it pretty bad. I don't suppose that simple, sorrowful truth has ever been given finer, more powerful expression than in *Oedipus the King*, where a baby is cast out to prevent it committing the ultimate horrors, but is rescued in order to grow up and commit them; where, grown to manhood and warned by a deceptive god, he runs from the place he thinks is his home to avoid killing the man he thinks is his father and sleeping with the woman he thinks is his mother, only to meet and murder his real father on his travels, and to marry and mate with his real mother at the end of them. This is sod's law writ large – writ heroic, if you will.

A word about the verse. I chose rhyming couplets for the scenes and varying rhyme/metrical schemes for the choruses. The first choice was made in the hope of giving the piece a kind of heightened quality – some sort of inadequate analogue for the wonderful sonority of the Greek. After all, there's nothing worse than bad *blank* verse, and bad is pretty much what I would have produced in that line. But I've tried to keep the *rhymes* simple, to avoid unwelcome titters. Along the same lines, the mix-and-match approach to the choruses is my stab at recreating the various lyrical forms that Sophocles employs.

RANJIT BOLT, 1996

OEDIPUS THE KING

CAST LIST

OEDIPUS THE KING recieved its British première in this version at the Royal National Theatre in September 1996. The cast was as follows:

OEDIPUS	ALAN HOWARD
PRIEST OF ZEUS	MICHAEL CARTER
CREON	PIP DONAGHY
TIRESIAS	GREG HICKS
JOCASTA	SUZANNE BERTISH
MESSENGER	SIMON SCOTT
SHEPHERD	PETER GORDON
SECOND MESSENGER	JEFFERY KISSOON
CHORUS/GROUP	JOHN BAXTER, JEAN-BENOIT BLANC, HELEN BOURNE, CHRISTIAN BURGESS, CHRISTOPHER CAMPBELL, TAMSIN DIVES, SOPHIE GRIMMER, COLIN HURLEY, KATHLEEN McGOLDRICK, TANYA MOODIE, GRAHAM SINCLAIR, JENNIE STOLLER, CLARE SWINBURNE
DIRECTOR	PETER HALL
DESIGNER	DIONYSIS FOTOPOULOS
LIGHTING	MARK HENDERSON
MUSIC	JUDITH WEIR

OEDIPUS THE KING

OEDIPUS: My children, latest harvest of the seed
That old king Cadmus sewed, what pressing need
Has brought you to me? Something grave it's clear:
Why else would you be sitting, silent here –
Bearing those branches, wreathed with woolly strands,
The signs of supplication, in your hands?
Our city reeks of incense; everywhere
Paeans and cries of anguish pierce the air.
I don't want messengers to tell me why,
And so I've come to you in person – I,
Illustrious Oedipus. Enlighten me,
Old man: by right of seniority
It's you that ought to speak for all the rest
What is it that you fear, or would request?
Depend on it, whatever I can do
I shall: I'm human and I pity you.

PRIEST: Oedipus, King of Thebes, there couldn't be
A more diverse assembly than you see
Before your altars now: we represent
All ages – some are priests like me; some bent
And bowed with age; some in their prime; and some
Children so small that they were scared to come
Without their mothers. Meanwhile, in the town,
Our fellow citizens are sitting down,
With branches in their hands, like this in mine,
In market-places, at Apollo's shrine
And near the temples of Athene. Why?
A sea of suffering has risen high
Above our heads – we're drowning in despair:
Crops fail; our flocks are dying everywhere;
Babies are *born* dead; and a plague's swooped down,
Spreading its hateful foulness through the town –
Laying it waste and loading countless biers –
While Hades gluts itself on groans and tears.
You're not the equal of the gods, we know,
But first among us mortals here below,
Both in life's everyday events and when
The gods loom large in the affairs of men.

Who freed us from the sphinx's clutches? You,
When first you came here – unassisted, too,
Or not by us: what *could* we do or say,
Ignorant as we were, to help you slay
The sphinx whose teasing song tormented us –
But they *do* say a god did. Oedipus,
Take *counsel* from a god or from a man –
Help us, great king, in any way you can.
When a man really knows life, as you do,
His plans succeed – at least they're likely to.
Ensure that, as your efforts years ago
Saw you saluted as our saviour, so
In times to come we won't recall your reign
As one that put us on our feet again
Only to fall more heavily – ensure
That our recovery is quite secure.
You brought good omens and good fortune then.
You must reverse the tide of death again.
What could an empty kingdom profit you?
Who would command a ship without a crew?

OEDIPUS: Oh my poor children! All your misery –
Let me assure you – is well known to me
But you could never suffer as I do.
The pain you feel is felt by each of you
And each alone – my grief's three times as great:
Grief for myself, for you and for the State.
Have I been sleeping all this while? Not so.
I've wept my fill; I want you all to know
How this has been exercising me.
After much thought a single remedy
Occurred to me, and this is what I've done:
Creon, my brother in-law, Menoiceus' son
Has gone to Delphi, to Apollo's shrine.
I sent him with this object: to divine
What it might be that we must do or say
To drive the plague from Thebes. He's been away
A long time now – this curious delay
Perplexes me. But when he does return,
I promise, it will be my sole concern
To carry out the god's commands to us –

Or else, revile the name of Oedipus.

PRIEST: That promise, Oedipus, could hardly be
             More timely: someone's signalling to me
             That Creon's here.

OEDIPUS: Apollo, may the light
             That's in his eyes reflect a hope as bright.

PRIEST: Would he be crowned with laurel otherwise?
             My hopes have certainly begun to rise.

OEDIPUS: We'll soon find out if we can trust that sign.
             What news, Creon, from Apollo's shrine?

CREON: The burden of our suffering's hard to bear
             But we may see an end to our despair.

OEDIPUS: What was the oracle? It isn't clear
             From those words whether we should hope or fear.

CREON: Perhaps you feel these people shouldn't hear.
             Shall we go in? It's all the same to me.

OEDIPUS: No – let them hear; I feel their pain, you see,
             More keenly than my own.

CREON: Then listen well:
             Apollo's order is that we expel
             Something that presently pollutes this land –
             Something we harbour here among us, and
             Whose taint no other course can nullify.

OEDIPUS: What cleansing rite must we perform, and why?

CREON: A man must be expelled, or his blood spilt
             In payment for the blood he shed: his guilt
             Is what's destroying Thebes.

OEDIPUS: Who is he, though?
             Who does Apollo mean?

CREON: Some time ago
               Laius was king here – he preceded you.

OEDIPUS: I've often heard the man alluded to –
               I never met him.

CREON: He was killed and *we*
               Must punish those, whoever they may be,
               Who killed him. Phoebus unequivocally
               Commands us to.

OEDIPUS: Where are they? Given the time
               That has elapsed since their appalling crime
               How can we trace them?

CREON: Well, Apollo said
               They're still in Thebes, and once the net is spread
               They can be caught.

OEDIPUS: Indeed. Where was the King
               When he was killed – at home or travelling?

CREON: He went to Delphi, and he did not come back.

OEDIPUS: Did anybody witness the attack –
               Someone with the king – or simply there –
               Whose report might well have led somewhere?

CREON: There *were* companions – they were butchered too;
               All except one, who fled the scene, and who
               Confirmed *one* thing.

OEDIPUS: Perhaps a vital clue
               Let's hear.

CREON: Some robbers fell on them. The king
               Was killed by many hands.

OEDIPUS: But anything
               So daring wouldn't have been done for free.
               Someone here paid the robbers.

CREON: Bribery.
           We did suspect that. In our dark time, though,
           We had nobody to help us.

OEDIPUS: Oh?
           So those times stopped you hunting high and low
           For clues? Hadn't these robbers killed a king?

CREON: The sphinx's riddle was the only thing
           That occupied us, overshadowing
           Less pressing matters.

OEDIPUS: We'll bring all to light.
           Apollo, and you too of course, are right
           To take up Laius' cause. He'll find in me
           A fitting ally, whose sole aim will be
           Vengeance for Thebes – and for Apollo, too.
           I'll wipe this taint away, I promise you –
           I'll do it, not for Laius' sake alone
           But also, or entirely, for my own,
           Since there's still a possibility
           That his assassins will come after me;
           It's in my interest to espouse his cause.
           Up, children – take away these boughs of yours.
           Summon the people – they'll be notified
           That I intend to leave no course untried.
           We shall drive the pestilence away
           With Phoebus' help, or founder.

PRIEST: *(to the others)*   Don't delay.
           He's said just what we wanted him to say.
           Phoebus, you sent this oracle: descend
           And save us. Bring the plague to a swift end.

CHORUS 1: What in the world can it have meant –
           This latest message that's been sent
           From Delphi from Apollo's shrine –
           To Thebes, a host of fears foment
           In this suffering soul of mine –
           Phoebus Apollo, doleful cries
           Are raised to you that rend the skies –

We beg you, send a sign
And say what cleansing rite,
Must be performed. We look to you:
Tell us what we have to do.

Athene, we appeal to you
And Artemis, your sister, who,
Enthroned above our market square,
Protects the town from there;
We call upon Apollo, too –
Who fires his arrows far and wide –
Three gods who form our triple shield
Against destruction – be revealed!
Appear now at our side!
When plagues were set to blast
This sacred city in the past
You have driven them away –
Do the same for us today!

Countless cares now weigh us down;
We can find no sure defence
Against the raging pestilence
That ravages the town.
Soil whose richness was well known
Is blighted, barren; women groan
In the pangs of childbirth – why,
When they, and their offspring, die?
Fast as a bird, as fire, lives flit away
To Death's grim shore, never again to see the light of day.

So the city perishes
While her people lie around,
Dead, and unmourned, on the ground.
But sickness flourishes.
Wives and white-haired mothers stand
Wailing at the altars and
Beg the gods to bring relief
At last – an end to pain and grief.
So prayers for health are mingled with laments –
Daughter of Zeus, Athene, rid us of this pestilence!

Death is ravaging us today
Let him leave us, say
For the Atlantic Ocean, or
The Black Sea's inhospitable shore.
Horror by night – horror with each new day.
Zeus – the father – in your hand you hold
The fiery lightning – take that bolt
And thunder with it, and blast death away.
Be our defender too, Phoebus.
Send arrows whizzing from your golden bowstring. Stand by us.
Artemis bring your torch, the one
You always carry as you run
Through the Lycian Mountains. And our cries
Go out to you – the Bacchae's drunken friend –
Dionysus – bring your torch and end
The reign of death – the god the gods despise.

Enter Oedipus.

OEDIPUS: I have the right response to your request:
              If you're prepared to do as I suggest
              You'll end the sickness – find relief. Well now
              My friends I no more knew precisely how
              Laius was killed than killed him – So you see
              I cannot hope to solve the mystery –
              Newcomer that I am – without some clue.
              For that, therefore, I now appeal to you –
              People of Thebes – to each and every one:
              If someone knows who murdered Laius, son
              Of Labdacus, I order him to say.
              Should he be frightened, as perhaps he may,
              If guilty of the crime, I'll calm his fear:
              I promise him that banishment from here –
              Nothing worse – will be the penalty.
              Or, if he knows the murderer to be
              A foreigner, let him declare that too.
              He'll get a rich reward, as is his due,
              And I shall be forever in his debt.
              But anyone who knows the truth and yet,
              To save his own skin or protect a friend,
              Conceals it – let him hear how I intend

To punish him: let no one anywhere
In *my* realm shelter him, or let him share
In sacrifices with them, or in prayer,
Or even speak to him. No, they must ban
That miscreant from their homes. For he's the man
Polluting Thebes. I wish him pain and strife –
May he lead a sorry, desolate life,
Wretch that he is. And for myself, I pray
That if, and with my knowledge, he (or they)
Should ever share my roof, then I too may
Suffer these penalties. That's my decree.
Enforce it and obey it, then – for me,
And for Apollo and, not least though last,
Our land, that angry Heaven chose to blast
With barrenness. For this is the gods' will.
But even if that weren't so, you should still
Have searched, and searched, and purged away the guilt
A king's blood – and a great one's – had been spilt.
His power is mine now. His queen shares my bed –
Received his seed – receives mine in its stead;
Also, if he'd lived long enough to see
That woman bear him children, there would be
More ties between us – offspring, mine and his,
Born of the self same womb, while, as it is,
Fate struck him down too soon for that – I say
For all these reasons I shall fight today
For him as for a father. Leave untried
No course, till I've tracked down the regicide.
The curse that I'm about to utter lies
On anyone who doesn't do likewise:
May the gods now blight their fields, and make
Their women barren, and may this plague take
Them off – or else some worse catastrophe.
As for the rest – for such as side with me:
May justice be their champion, and may
The gods go with them till their dying day.

CHORUS: Oedipus, since I face your curse, hear this:
                I'm not the murderer, and who he is
                I couldn't say. Since Phoebus set us on
                To make this search, let him, if anyone,

Reveal who did the deed.

OEDIPUS: You're right, of course.
But no man on this earth can ever force
A god to act against his will.

CHORUS: Quite so.
There is another course of action, though.

OEDIPUS: I'm ready to assess all remedies.

CHORUS: Who sees as clearly as Apollo sees –
Or nearly so? The priest, Tiresias, sire.
And anyone who wishes to inquire
Into this mystery ought to gain a true
And clear account of it from him.

OEDIPUS: This, too,
I have considered. Creon prompted me –
I sent a man for him – two men – but he
(And this amazes me) does not appear.

CHORUS: Without him we have nothing but unclear,
All but forgotten rumours.

OEDIPUS: Tell me more.
There *is* no information I'll ignore.

CHORUS: They say some vagabonds killed the king.

OEDIPUS: I know.
Nobody here has seen the culprit, though.

CHORUS: The culprit's heard your curse. He'll soon appear
And speak up – if he's capable of fear.

OEDIPUS: One must be bold to do what that man's done.
Words won't frighten him.

CHORUS: But here comes one
Who *can* convict him: they have brought him here –

Tiresias – that great – that god-like seer:
Among us men, truth lives in him alone.

Enter Tiresias, led by a Boy.

OEDIPUS: Tiresias, to whom all things are known –
What may and what may not be spoken of
Concerning earth below and heaven above –
I know you sense, although you cannot see,
The plague now plunging Thebes in misery.
Great prophet, we must look to you to save
Our city – you're the only hope we have.
For Phoebus (if you haven't heard by now)
In answer to our question, told us how
The sickness might be driven from our town:
This can't be done, except by tracking down
And either killing, or else banishing
The man who murdered Laius, our late king.
Now, with your knowledge of the birds' cries, or
Some other craft contained in see-ers' law,
Save the city, and yourself, and me.
Ward the miasma off – the legacy
Of the dead man. We all depend on you.
What is the noblest thing a man can do
If not to assist his fellow man
In any and in every way he can.

TIRESIAS: Oh, it is truly terrible to be wise
With wisdom in which no advantage lies.
I knew that – knew it well – but I forgot,
Or I would not have come here now.

OEDIPUS: Why not?
Something has saddened you – please tell us what.

TIRESIAS: Let me go home. Your load and mine will weigh
That much less if you let me.

OEDIPUS: What you say
Isn't lawful, and it's hostile, too,
To this city, which has nurtured you.

I asked a question – will you not reply?

TIRESIAS: *You've* spoken rashly. Heaven forbid that I
Should make the same mistake.

OEDIPUS: Tiresias, please –
We're begging you – we're all but on our knees.
Don't forsake us – tell us what you know.

TIRESIAS: You're fools! *(to Oedipus)* I'll hide what gives me pain, and so
Steer clear of causing *you* pain.

OEDIPUS: Oh? What's this?
You know but will not say? Your purpose is
To destroy Thebes? Forsake her citizens?

TIRESIAS: To quiz me on this question makes no sense.
I'm avoiding *your* pain and my own.
I'll tell you nothing.

OEDIPUS: You'd enrage a stone,
Wickedest of the wicked! Must you be
Unbending – useless?

TIRESIAS: You find fault with me –
You blame *my* temper – what about your own?

OEDIPUS: Who'd not be angry, when you take that tone
And spit upon this city?

TIRESIAS: Yet, although
I'm silent, it will come.

OEDIPUS: And since that's so
Speak.

TIRESIAS: No. I cannot. Vent your rage on me.

OEDIPUS: I shall. Hear this, then: you were obviously
The chief accomplice in the crime – in fact
All but committed that barbaric act.

I'd say you'd done so, too, if you could see.

TIRESIAS: Enough. Then, king, obey your own decree.
From this day forward, speak to nobody.
You are the man who now pollutes this land.

OEDIPUS: Shameless! Inventing tales like that! You'll pay
For this.

TIRESIAS: No. Truth is strength, and what I say
Is true.

OEDIPUS: Who set you on to say it, though?
You didn't read that in some entrails.

TIRESIAS: No.
You set me on. Forced me to speak.

OEDIPUS: Again!
Repeat it! I'll have grasped it fully then.

TIRESIAS: Didn't I make my meaning crystal clear?
Or are you testing me?

OEDIPUS: Just let me hear
Those words again. I haven't *grasped* them yet.

TIRESIAS: This manhunt – *you're* the man.

OEDIPUS: You *will* regret
Repeating treason!

TIRESIAS: Shall I anger you
Further? "Invent" another "tale"?

OEDIPUS: Yes! Do!
Waste more breath.

TIRESIAS: I *will* do: you defile
Your flesh and blood: oblivious the while,
You wallow with them in the foulest sin,

Ignorant of the peril you are in.

OEDIPUS: You think you can come out with lies like this
And not pay.

TIRESIAS: If there's strength in truth.

OEDIPUS: There *is* –
Except for you, Tiresias, you're blind –
Not only in your eyes but in your mind.

TIRESIAS: The taunts you fling at me, you'll shortly find,
Flung by all Thebes at *you*. Poor wretch!

OEDIPUS: Your sight
Has been replaced by an eternal night.
Should I, or anyone who sees the light,
Fear *you*?

TIRESIAS: It's for Apollo, not for me,
To strike you down. That is your destiny.

OEDIPUS: Who made all this up? Not Creon?

TIRESIAS: No –
Creon's not your enemy – *you* are.

OEDIPUS: Oh,
Wealth, power, my mind – a mind so very fine!
How envious men are of a life like mine!
What hatred it incurs! To get the crown
Given me by the people of this town –
Not sought by me – a man I trust – Creon –
My friend – creeps up on me, intent upon
Ousting me, and, of all accomplices,
Suborns a scheming charlatan like this –
A cunning beggar whose sole thought is gain
Ignorant of his art – that much is plain:
(to Tiresias) Tell me: in what sense are *you* a seer?
Why was it, when the singing dog was here,
That *you* said nothing that could set Thebes free?

Expound that riddle? No one ordinary
Could do it. It required a *seer*. You knew
Nothing – no bird, no god, would teach it you.
Ignorant Oedipus comes along and hits
The target – and with what? Only his wits –
Only his wits – no bird instructed *me*!
You're out to oust me now – you think you'll be
Well in with Creon, and stand by his throne.
This bid to "purify" Thebes will cost the one
Who launched it, *and* you, dear. If *you* weren't old
You'd pay a terrible price for being so bold.

CHORUS: He speaks in anger – as do you, my king.
There's no occasion here for quarrelling.
How can we carry out the god's command?
That is the business we now have in hand.

TIRESIAS: King though you are, I've the same right you have
To speak – and say as much, too. I'm the slave
Of Phoebus – not you. What I *will* not be
Is counted Creon's creature. *You* mocked *me*
For being blind, but, sighted though you are –
Yes, eyes and all – you fail to see how far
You've gone in evil, being unaware
Of where you live, or who lives *with* you there.
Who are your parents? Do you know? Or know
How you have wronged your closest kin below –
Yes, *and* above the earth? Or how, one day,
You will be forced to fly Thebes, chased away
By a dire, double, sure curse, laid on you
By both your parents; seeing darkness, too,
Though now you "see the light"? And all around
Cithaeron, cries of anguish will resound –
Your cries, *your* anguish, Oedipus, when you've found...
Yes, once you've understood just what you've done
By marrying – fouled your house. That haven – one
You sailed so smoothly into – there was none
More treacherous. Other evils you don't see
Will smash you and your children. So heap *me*
And what I say, and Creon too, with scorn –
More miserable than any mortal born,

You shall be crushed.

OEDIPUS: Why must he cross me so?
(to Tiresias) Destruction take you! Leave my palace! Go!
At once!

TIRESIAS: I came because you sent for me.

OEDIPUS: Had I but reckoned with the idiocy
Of your pronouncements I would not have.

TIRESIAS: Oh!
An idiot, am I? Maybe *you* think so –
Your parents didn't...

OEDIPUS: What?! Parents you say?
"My parents didn't think so"? Who were they?

TIRESIAS: This very day you will discover who –
This is the day that will destroy you too.

OEDIPUS: You baffle me with riddles.

TIRESIAS: Riddles, eh?
They're what you solve so easily, aren't they?

OEDIPUS: You mock the mind that won – *will win* the day.

TIRESIAS: That stroke of luck's destroyed you.

OEDIPUS: Should I care?
I saved this city.

TIRESIAS: I must go. You there –
Boy – come with me and guide me.

OEDIPUS: Let him, then.
And maybe I shall have some peace again.

TIRESIAS: I'll say exactly what I came to say –
Then take my leave. So lower and scowl away –

I'm not afraid. *You* can't hurt *me*. Hear this:
You wonder where the man you're hunting is?
The man your proclamation was about –
The killer, whom you're threatening to cast out?
He's here – a foreigner, or so we thought;
Sadly he is nothing of the sort;
Oh, how the wretch will grieve when it is shown
That he's a native of this very town!
Blind to the world that, till today, he saw –
No longer rich and powerful but poor –
He'll have to leave this city, staff in hand,
Tapping his course off to a foreign land.
It will be found that he's his children's brother
As well as father, husband to his mother
As well as son, and took his father's life,
And shares a bed now with his father's *wife*.
Go in. Think *that* through. If you find me wrong
Then say my prophesies aren't worth a song.

CHORUS 2:   From Delphi's holy rock there came a voice:
"The foulest murder has been done!" Who by?
Whose hands are stained with blood? He has no choice:
Faster than fast horses he must fly.
Apollo son of Zeus,
Armed with fire and lightning, now pursues
The guilty man; the fates go with him; they
Will catch their prey.

From Mount Parnassus, with its snowy peak,
The message flashed out: "Find the nameless one!"
On rocks, in caves and wild woods, we must seek
This man, who limps along, sad and alone,
His desperate aim
To flee the fearful oracle that came
From earth's core; but it buzzes round him still,
As gadflies will.

The see-er's wise. His prophesy has filled my soul with fear.
I don't believe or disbelieve him – what am I to say?
I'm filled with fresh anxieties: the past is still unclear –
The present too. There was no feud, nor is there one today,

Between the house of Oedipus and that of Laius – none
Ever, that *I* know of, or that might be evidence
Against illustrious Oedipus, to show that he's the one
Who killed the late king, and to make him pay for his offence.

Apollo is omniscient; all the affairs of men
Are known to him, but does a seer see more than me and you?
Who knows? We may be wiser one way, he another. When,
But not *until* Tiresias' words are proven to be true
Shall I agree with any who accuse king Oedipus.
What of the sphinx? We saw the man confront her, didn't we?
He passed the test. It was his wits alone that rescued us.
He'll never be accused of *any* crime – or not by *me*.

Enter Creon.

CREON: I am outraged. Oedipus has laid
            Dire charges at my door. If he's afraid
            That in the present troubles, I, Creon,
            Wronged him in word or deed, can life go on?
            Why should it? No, my friends, I'd rather die
            Than live with blame like that, and this is why:
            His words must hurt me in more ways than one –
            Think of the damage that they will have done
            If I should be accused of treachery,
            And you, my friends, all Thebes, think *that* of me?

CHORUS: He made the charge but maybe what he said
            Rage prompted, and the heart spoke not the head.

CREON: He said the seer was *my* pawn?

CHORUS: He said so.
            He wasn't thinking when he said it, though.

CREON: And when he charged me with this, did he seem
            Quite sane? Or could you see the tell-tale gleam
            Of madness in his eyes?

CHORUS: I couldn't say.
            A king is hard to fathom? Anyway

He's coming out.

Enter Oedipus.

OEDIPUS: You! What's your business here?
How dare you! What effrontery! To appear
Before my doors, when anyone can see
That *you* killed Laius; now you're cheating me
Out of my kingdom. Are you doing this
Because you've seen some sign of cowardice
Or folly in me? Did you count on stealth?
Or think I'd see, but not defend myself?
Stupid! So stupid, to attempt alone
What calls for wealth and followers! A throne
Is seldom seized without them.

CREON: Think the worst
By all means, when you've heard – but listen first.

OEDIPUS: You're a smooth talker. Since you're hostile to me
What good can your account of matters do me?

CREON: Listen to this first. Let me speak.

OEDIPUS: Do so.
Don't tell me that you're not a traitor though.

CREON: If you believe that stubbornness combined
With folly is a boon, you've lost your mind.

OEDIPUS: If you believe you're licensed to offend
So close a kinsman, *you've* lost *yours,* my friend.

CREON: Of course I've no such licence. But you say
I've done you wrong. Just tell me in what way.

OEDIPUS: Who was it made me have them bring the seer,
That oh-so-reverend entrail-reader, here?

CREON: Me. I'm convinced it was a good idea.

OEDIPUS: How long since Laius...?

CREON: Go on.

OEDIPUS: ... met his end.

CREON: Years. Yes, an age ago.

OEDIPUS: Our prophet friend –
Was he practising his mystery then?

CREON: Yes. He was – with equal skill, and men
Held him in no less awe.

OEDIPUS: Did he let fall
Nothing concerning me?

CREON: Nothing at all.
Not in my hearing, anyway.

OEDIPUS: I see –
You looked for Laius' killers?

CREON: Naturally.
But we learned nothing.

OEDIPUS: This "skilled" prophet, though,
Said nothing *then*. Why not?

CREON: I wouldn't know.
It's always been my custom to remain
Silent concerning what I can't explain.

OEDIPUS: One thing you *should* explain. One thing you know.

CREON: What? I shall tell you freely, if that's so.

OEDIPUS: This: that the two of you colluded. Why,
Otherwise, would he allege that *I*
Had murdered Laius?

CREON: He said *that,* did he?
I'll take your word for it. It's news to me.
I've answered *you.* Now answer *me.*

OEDIPUS: Go on,
Ask. Ask. It *won't* be shown that I'm the one
Who murdered Laius.

CREON: Well now, tell me this
My sister is your wife?

OEDIPUS: Why, so she is.
I can't deny that fact.

CREON: And with joint sway
You rule this land?

OEDIPUS: I let her have her way
In everything.

CREON: And I'm your partner? Yes?
We three share power?

OEDIPUS: Which makes your fickleness
All the more wounding.

CREON: I'm not fickle, though.
Think clearly, like me, and you'll see that's so.
First, who would look for power that must destroy
His peace of mind, if able to enjoy
That power without fear, sleeping peacefully?
I exercise a king's authority –
Kingship itself has never tempted me.
Nor would it *any* wise man in my shoes.
For were I king of Thebes I couldn't choose
But act against my will, and often too;
Whereas, at present, I receive from you
Whatever I desire, with no unease.
Could kingship better benefits like these?
Influence free from all anxieties?
A ruler's scope without the cares he knows?

The only honours I desire are those
That profit me. I'm not a fool, you see.
Everyone in this city flatters me.
Anyone wanting something from you, say,
Comes to confer with *me,* and why do they?
I can see they get no matter what:
Whyever would I wish to change my lot
For yours, or join in someone else's plot?
For proof of this, first go to Delphi – there
Ask what Apollo said – discover where
I misreported him. And second, find
There was complicity of any kind
Between me and the seer. And if you *do*
Condemn me – yes, to *death* – I'll vote with you.
But just your vague assumptions cannot be
A proper basis for accusing me.
It's wrong, when there's no reason why you should,
To think good friends are bad – or bad ones good.
To spurn a friend – I mean a friend that's true –
Is like rejecting what's most dear to you –
That's life itself. You'll come to comprehend,
The truth of this in time, and in the end
The just man's always proven to be so;
The unjust man takes but a day to know.

CHORUS: *(to Oedipus)* Wise words indeed. Pay heed to them, my son,
              Or court catastrophe.

OEDIPUS: A plot's begun –
              Quickly, too – against me. Must I not –
              And just as quickly – hatch a counterplot?
              Suppose I simply waited quietly?
              Who'd succeed? Me or my enemy?

CREON: What do you want to do, then? Banish me?

OEDIPUS: No. It's death for you.

CREON: From what you say
              It seems you won't believe me, or give way.
              I can see that you're... not sane.

OEDIPUS: Not so.
            I watch my interests.

CREON: And should watch mine.

OEDIPUS: No.
            You're a traitor.

CREON: What if *you're* a fool?

OEDIPUS: I must rule.

CREON: So you must. But don't *mis*rule.

OEDIPUS: The city!

CREON: *I'm* a citizen, like you,

CHORUS: *(seeing Jocasta come out of the palace)*
            Jocasta – and a timely entrance, too –
            Stop – let her make your peace.

JOCASTA: What? Quarrelling?
            Wretched men! Over some silly thing?
            For shame! An argument – a private one –
            And the town gripped by plague. Go home, Creon –
            (to Oedipus) Come into the palace. *(to both)* Don't create
            Great conflicts out of things that have no weight.

CREON: Sister, your husband has been threatening me
            With banishment or death.

OEDIPUS: Yes. Because he,
            I find, has schemed against me.

CREON: No. Not I.
            May I never thrive in life, but die
            Accursed, if I've done anything to you –
            If a single charge you've made is true.

JOCASTA: *(to Oedipus)* Believe him, Oedipus, believe him – both

Because you should respect his terrible oath –
That first – but also for their sakes *(indicates Chorus)* and mine.

CHORUS: *(to Oedipus)*
Listen, I beg of you. Reflect, and rather than decline...

OEDIPUS: You want some favour? Tell me what it is.

CHORUS: Respect the oath he's sworn. Respect great wisdom such as his.

OEDIPUS: What is it that you want from me? Please make your
meaning clear.

CHORUS: Don't accuse a friend because you have a vague idea
He might be guilty. And the oath he swore
Was solemn – sacred.

OEDIPUS: What you're asking for –
Since I must make you understand
Is this: my exile from the land,
If not my death.

CHORUS: No – by the greatest of the gods – the sun:
Let *me* die, and my death be one
To shudder at – with not one friend –
Forsaken by the gods above, if that's what I intend.
But I'm in despair:
The pestilence that rages everywhere
Sickens my soul, as does the thought that now the two of you
Compound old griefs with new.

OEDIPUS: Let him go free, then, though it means that I
Must be disgraced and banished, or else die.
Your words have won me round – *his never* can.
No matter where he is, I'll hate the man.

CREON: You do submit, *then* – but with sullenness –
Just as you carried anger to excess:
Rancour replaces rage. Such natures, though,
Must cause *themselves* most pain, and justly so.

OEDIPUS: Will you not leave me now? I beg you, go!

CREON: I'm going. But your judgement is awry,
            I'm in the right, as they can testify.

            He indicates the Chorus and Jocasta, then goes.

CHORUS: *(to Jocasta)* Won't you take Oedipus inside?

JOCASTA: I'll do so by and by.
            First I need to know what's happened here.

CHORUS: Something came up in conversation – an absurd idea –
            But a false charge *can* wound.

JOCASTA: Are both to blame?

CHORUS: I fear they are.

JOCASTA: What *was* this talk?

CHORUS: The business has already gone too far.
            I think it would be best to leave things be.
            It's Thebes I'm thinking of.

OEDIPUS: Neglecting *me*.
            I used to think your judgement was so good,
            And now you're trying to calm my angry mood.

CHORUS: Have I not said before, it would be madness, Oedipus,
            To spurn a man who rescued us
            Before, and from as dire a fate
            As ever threatened my beloved Thebes; who'll steer our State,
            With Heaven's help, once more
            To safety's seemingly far-distant shore.
            You brought salvation to us in the midst of horror. How
            Can we reject you now?

JOCASTA: Tell me, Oedipus – I too must know:
            What can it be that has incensed you so?

OEDIPUS: Since I respect you more than them *(meaning Chorus)* Creon –
            Has started a conspiracy...

JOCASTA: Go on –
            Give me a full account, and a clear one.

OEDIPUS: He claims that *I* killed Laius.

JOCASTA: His proof, though –
            Hearsay? Or his own knowledge?

OEDIPUS: Neither. No,
            He sent a lying prophet so that *he,*
            Even as he incriminated me,
            Might not be seen to do so.

JOCASTA: Have no fear:
            You're innocent, as I shall make quite clear.
            Yes, I have proof as sure as proof can be
            That no man has the gift of prophesy.
            Laius received an oracle long ago
            It came not from Apollo, as I'll show,
            But from a seer of his, who claimed to see
            That a son – a son he'd have by me
            Would murder him. Yet that was not the case.
            A band of robbers killed him, at a place
            Where three roads meet, we're told. And, furthermore,
            Our son was barely three days old before
            Laius gave orders for him to be cast
            Among the rocks, where travellers never passed –
            His ankles pinned together. So you see,
            It *wasn't* the Gods' will that he should be
            His father's killer, or that Laius die
            As he had feared he would do, murdered by
            His son. Yet these events were what the seer
            Foretold, and that should give you some idea
            What little heed you owe the prophesy.
            For what Apollo wants accomplished, he
            And only he makes manifest – with ease.

OEDIPUS: Woman, what terrible anxieties

Your words have started in me.

JOCASTA: In what way
Have I alarmed you?

OEDIPUS: Did I hear you say
That Laius was – was murdered at a spot
Where three roads meet?

JOCASTA: That's the report we got.
It's still said.

OEDIPUS: Where?

JOCASTA: Phocis. Where roads that lead
From Dauli-a and Delphi meet.

OEDIPUS: Indeed?
How long ago was this?

JOCASTA: We heard the news
Shortly before your reign began.

OEDIPUS: Oh, Zeus,
What monstrous fate had you in mind for me?

JOCASTA: What can the cause of this strange anguish be?
Oedipus, tell me.

OEDIPUS: Now is not the time.
How old was Laius? Was he in his prime?
What did he look like? Well?

JOCASTA: Very like you.
His hair was turning grey, or starting to.

OEDIPUS: Wretch! I've cursed my*self*, unwittingly.

JOCASTA: What is it, Oedipus? You're frightening me.

OEDIPUS: I'm terrified. Perhaps the see-er saw.

To make this clear I *must* know one thing more.

JOCASTA: I'll tell it you, despite my terror.

OEDIPUS: Then
Was Laius travelling with a few men,
Or with a troop of soldiers, like a king?

JOCASTA: Well, there was a wagon carrying
Laius; a herald; and three others.

OEDIPUS: So –
It's crystal clear. Who told you all this, though?

JOCASTA: A slave – the only one to get away.

OEDIPUS: Where is he now? Here?

JOCASTA: No. The very day
The man returned to Thebes, discovering
That you had solved the riddle and were king,
He took my hand – began petitioning
To be sent to the fields, with the idea
Of getting just as far away from here
As possible. His service had been such
Nothing he asked for could have been too much.
I sent him.

OEDIPUS: Get him back, and quickly too.

JOCASTA: All right, but what use can he be to you?

OEDIPUS: I fear I've spoken rashly, which is why
I want to see him.

JOCASTA: So you shall. But I
Deserve to know what you're so troubled by.

OEDIPUS: All right. My fears are mounting. Who is there
With such a right to hear, and who could share
In my distress as you do? You're aware

That I'm the son of Polybus; that he
Is king of Corinth, and that Merope,
Who claims descent from Dorus, is his queen.
Now, Corinth was a city where I'd been
Revered by everybody. Then, one day,
A strange thing happened – I myself would say
It angered me unduly – anyway,
At a feast a drunken diner said,
As the wine went swiftly to his head,
That I was not my father's son. And I,
Despite my indignation, which was high,
Restrained myself, though far from easily,
For that day. But the next I went to see
My parents – questioned them at length. And they
Made the author of this slander pay
Dearly for it. From this, at least, I drew
Some comfort. Yet the taunt, as taunts will do,
Vexed me, and constant brooding kept it new.
Without my parents' knowledge, I set out
For Delphi, where, on what I asked about,
The God was silent, though he did reply.
What he foretold my soul was harrowed by,
For it was truly terrible: he said
My fate was to defile my mother's bed;
To show mankind a brood that it would rather
Be blind than look on; and to kill my father.
I heard, was horrified, and after that
Kept clear of Corinth, sometimes gazing at
The stars above it – knowing it was there –
But certain I must shun a city where
That fearful prophesy might be fulfilled.
I travelled through the land where he was killed –
Laius, that is – if what you say is true.
Now, wife, I won't hide anything from you:
As I approached a place where three roads meet
A covered wagon drew near – on the seat
A man who looked like me, hair turning grey;
There was a herald. Pushed out of the way
I was. The one who'd pushed me I then hit.
The old man saw this and requited it
As I drew level with him, striking me

With his goad, on the head. The penalty
He paid for *that* was *not* a light one. No –
I struck him with my stick – a lethal blow
That sent him toppling down from where he sat
High up inside the wagon. After that
I killed them all. That stranger, though – if *he*
Was Laius, then there can be nobody
More cursed, more hated by the gods than me:
I'm to receive no hospitality,
No one's to speak to me. From every door
I must now be chased away. What's more
I myself pronounced the curse that I,
And I alone, am thus afflicted by.
I killed your king but, worse still, now he's dead
I have his queen and so pollute his bed.
See how the gods heap curses on my head,
If I must flee my *new* home, while my *old*
Is barred to me, since it has been foretold
That I'm going to marry Merope
My mother; kill the man who gave to me
The gift of life – who raised me: Polybus.
You would be right to pity Oedipus –
Wouldn't you? And to wonder if some power,
Divine and pitiless, saw fit to shower
These evils on him? Holy gods, I pray
That I may never see the evil day
But vanish from the earth first – never see
Such shame, such utter misery light on me.

CHORUS: This is terrible, yes, but don't despair –
            Not till you've heard from someone who was there.

OEDIPUS: We're still waiting for the shepherd. Yes –
            All *cannot* be entirely comfortless –
            Not yet, at any rate.

JOCASTA: And why is *he*
            Essential now?

OEDIPUS: Should his account agree
            With yours, all guilt is lifted from my head.

JOCASTA: What was so notable in what I said?

OEDIPUS: He told you robbers murdered Laius – no?
              Let him just repeat that this was so –
              That more than one man killed him, and I'm not –
              How *could* I be the murderer – can a lot –
              Can *more than one* be one? But if he says
              With certainty it *was* one man, then yes,
              We find the finger pointing at me.

JOCASTA: Well,
              That was the story all Thebes heard him tell.
              He surely can't deny it now, although,
              Were he to do so, he could still not show
              That Laius' son had killed him – that he died
              The death Apollo's "prophet" prophesied.
              My child was long since lost, poor innocent,
              When Laius died. No credence should be lent
              To any prophesy.

OEDIPUS: True. Nonetheless,
              Send somebody to fetch the shepherd.

JOCASTA: Yes.
              I shall – at once. But now let's go inside.
              Nothing that you demand must be denied.

CHORUS 3:   In everything I do and say
              I'll solemnly obey
              Those sacred laws that had their birth
              In Heaven, not on earth.
              They are immortal and sublime –
              Until the end of time
              They will endure. They are divine;
              Supreme; what praise is mine
              (I hope that I shall win it, too)
              Will certainly be due
              To the reverence I have shown
              For *them* – to that alone.

              In rampant arrogance we see

The root of tyranny:
It gluts itself on power and wealth
And so destroys itself;
Will scale the dizziest heights, and then
Plunge headlong down again.
And yet
I ask the gods to let
Ambition thrive –
The sort that keeps the city state alive
But our true champions are the gods, I know –
I'll never cease to think that's so.

If any man is arrogant in what he says and does –
Grudges the gods the worship due to them, and shows no fear
Of Justice, may he meet the evilest of ends, and thus
Pay for his fatal pride. He overreaches – cannot steer
Clear of unholy acts, but touches what he shouldn't touch.
While things like this are happening, who can confidently say
The angry gods will spare him? And if what men get for such
Conduct is honour, why should gods be worshipped anyway.

I'll never go to Delphi, to Apollo's shrine again;
Never to Abae's temple, or Olympia either – no,
Unless old prophesies are proven true, enabling men
To point to them and say: "It was foretold and it was so."
Take note of this, eternally omnipotent Zeus – the king
(If we're right to call you that): an oracle – the one
Given to Laius seems mistaken; they're dishonouring
Apollo, and the power of religion's all but gone.

Enter Jocasta and Servant.

JOCASTA: Incense and garlands. I shall go with these
To the temple. Oedipus' anxieties
Have reached a fever pitch. It's in the light
Of past events that new ones are judged right –
And judge them right is what he *will* not do.
The wildest arguments are listened to –
He seizes on the slightest grounds for fear.
To my advice he's turning a deaf ear.
And so, Apollo, since your altar's near,

I come to you, a suppliant, carrying
Tokens of prayer, and begging you to bring
An end to the pollution. Oedipus,
Our helmsman's overboard. That frightens us.

Enter Messenger.

MESSENGER: Friends, I'm a stranger – tell me, if you will,
Where Oedipus' palace is, or better still,
Where he himself is.

CHORUS: That's his palace there,
And he himself's at home. This woman here's
His queen. The mother of his children.

MESSENGER: Yes?
Then may she always know great happiness,
Both she and hers, since she's his queen.

JOCASTA: May *you,*
Likewise, my friend – and you deserve it, too,
For those kind words. But do you want something?
Is that why you've come? Or do you bring
Some news?

MESSENGER: I have good news for all of you –
Your house, your husband...

JOCASTA: What is it, and who
Has sent you?

MESSENGER: Corinth. And what I'm to tell
Will make you glad – it must – but sad as well,
I dare say.

JOCASTA: What *is* it?! How can there be
This double force to it?

MESSENGER: Apparently
The Corinthians will make him king.

JOCASTA: I see:
          Is Polybus not in power now?

MESSENGER: No. He's dead.

JOCASTA: Oedipus' father, gone? What have you said?

MESSENGER: I deserve to die if it's not true.

JOCASTA: *(to Servant)* Go in at once and tell your master.

           Servant goes.

                                                You!

           Oracles! Where are you now? For years
           Oedipus avoids this man, he fears
           He's going to murder him. And now he's died
           A natural death. There *is* no parricide.

           Enter Oedipus.

OEDIPUS: Jocasta, my dear wife, you sent for me?
           What is it, then?

JOCASTA: This man has news. You'll see,
           When you have heard it, how they stand today –
           The "awesome" oracles of the gods.

OEDIPUS: First say
           Who the man is – then what his message is.

JOCASTA: He's come from Corinth and he's told me this:
           Polybus, your father's dead.

OEDIPUS: *(to Messenger)*   What? I must hear
           This news from *you,* friend?

MESSENGER: Then I'll make it clear:
           Polybus *is* dead.

OEDIPUS: Murdered? Some disease?

MESSENGER: The old are frail and slight infirmities
            Can finish them.

OEDIPUS: It was some illness, then.

MESSENGER: It was – and age.

OEDIPUS: Wife, why indeed should men
            Look to Apollo's shrine, or heed the cries
            Of birds that scream above us in the skies?
            They told me I would kill my father. Why,
            He's dead and buried now – and here am I –
            How could I be the man? Of course, he *may*
            Have died of grief because I'd stayed away –
            In which case one could claim I killed him. Still,
            Oracles hold *no* truth and *never* will:
            They're buried *with* him. They are worthless.

JOCASTA: Yes.
            I told you that before, though.

OEDIPUS: I confess
            I was misled by fear.

JOCASTA: Now clear your head
            Of these misgivings.

OEDIPUS: But my mother's bed
            I *may* defile yet – rid me of *that* fear.

JOCASTA: Our lives are ruled by chance – we've no idea
            What is to come. To live from day to day –
            Fear nothing – that is best. Why dread you may
            Defile your mother's bed? Things of that kind
            Occur in dreams. Dismiss them from your mind –
            Such is the easiest way to live by far.

OEDIPUS: Wise words, Jocasta – I can see they are –
            But while my mother lives I'll be afraid.
            I've *no* choice.

JOCASTA: But your fears have been allayed –
Or largely – by your father's death.

JOCASTA: I know.
The fact remains my mother's living, though.

MESSENGER: Who is the woman who perturbs you so?

OEDIPUS: Merope – Polybus's wife.

MESSENGER: And why?

OEDIPUS: An oracle that I was frightened by
Was sent to me by Phoebus.

MESSENGER: Saying what?
Would it be right to tell me that?

OEDIPUS: *Why not?*
The god informed me that it was my fate
Both to kill my father and to mate
With my own mother. Therefore, from that day,
I kept away from Corinth – far away –
Long years away, that have been kind to me,
Although, of course, all children love to see
Their parents, more than anyone.

MESSENGER: These fears, then,
Were keeping you from coming home again?

OEDIPUS: Yes.

MESSENGER: Let me at once *unburden* you
Of fear, then, since I've come in friendship.

OEDIPUS: Do,
And you'll be well rewarded.

MESSENGER: I came here
Mainly because I *did* have an idea
That, when you returned, I'd stand to gain.

OEDIPUS: No – I'm never going home again.
                Back to my mother? No.

MESSENGER: Then I can see
                You're in the dark, my son.

OEDIPUS: Enlighten me.

MESSENGER: Your parents are the reason why you've stayed
                Away from home?

OEDIPUS: Exactly. I'm afraid
                That what Apollo said might well be true.

MESSENGER: That pollution might be brought on you
                By your parents?

OEDIPUS: That's my constant fear.

MESSENGER: Don't you know this dread of yours is mere
                Misguided nonsense?

OEDIPUS: Oh? That's far from clear
                If they're my parents.

MESSENGER: Polybus was *not*
                Your father – even your *relation*.

OEDIPUS: What?!
                Polybus not my father?

MESSENGER: No. No more
                Than I am.

OEDIPUS: But he called me son – what for?

MESSENGER: Well, I gave you to him long ago.

OEDIPUS: A gift! And he adored me even so?

MESSENGER: Because he had no child.

OEDIPUS: You bought me, then,
                    Or found me – which?

MESSENGER: I found you – in a glen
                    On Mount Cithaeron.

OEDIPUS: Mount Citheron, eh?
                    What were doing up there, anyway?

MESSENGER: Tending flocks.

OEDIPUS: You were a hireling.

MESSENGER: True.
                    I was a hireling – but I rescued you.

OEDIPUS: From what predicament did you "rescue" me?

MESSENGER: Just look at your ankles and you'll see.

OEDIPUS: You've recalled that old affliction – why?

MESSENGER: They'd been spiked together – it was I
                    Who set you free.

OEDIPUS: From earliest infancy
                    The stigma of those ankles stayed with me.

MESSENGER: And that was what you took your name from, too:
                    Oedipus – "Swollen Feet".

OEDIPUS: I beg of you,
                    If someone did this to me, tell me who.
                    Was it my father or my mother, man?

MESSENGER: That I couldn't tell you. Someone *can*.
                    The man who gave you to me then.

OEDIPUS: I see:
                    I was passed on to you by somebody.
                    You weren't in fact the one who found me.

MESSENGER: No.
             I got you from another shepherd.

OEDIPUS: Oh?
             Who was he? Can you tell me that one thing?

MESSENGER: They said he worked for Laius.

OEDIPUS: For the king
             Who used to rule Thebes many years ago?

MESSENGER: For him, yes.

OEDIPUS: Is this man alive? If so
             I'd give a lot to meet him.

MESSENGER: Who would know
             If not you Thebans?

OEDIPUS: Is that shepherd known
             To you, friends? Have you seen him in the town
             Or in some pasture? Please – I *have* to know.

CHORUS: He's the self–same shepherd... I think so...
             The one you were on tenterhooks to see –
             But ask Jocasta: she knows more than me.

OEDIPUS: You know the man we've sent for – *are* these two
             One and the same?

JOCASTA: Forget it. Why pursue
             The matter? Why not let the whole thing go?

OEDIPUS: When clues like these have come my way? Oh no:
             I'll solve the riddle of my birth today.

JOCASTA: I beg you, *don't* pursue this – anyway,
             Not if your life means anything to you.
             My misery's enough.

OEDIPUS: Don't worry. True,

My mother, and her mother, and hers too
May have been slaves, or worse. That wouldn't mean
That *you* were one jot lower than a queen.

JOCASTA: Please – husband – *don't* pursue this.

OEDIPUS: I won't *hear*
Of leaving off till everything is clear.

JOCASTA: I'm begging you to do what's best for you –
Because I love you.

OEDIPUS: All that I've been through,
My *misery's* come from what was "best" for me.

JOCASTA: Poor, hapless Oedipus! May you never see
Just who you are.

OEDIPUS: Will someone go and bring
That shepherd here? Jocasta's glorying
In her noble birth. Well, let her, then.

JOCASTA: Oh, Zeus! You're the wretchedest of men.
That's all I have to say. From this time on
I shall not speak.

CHORUS: Why has the lady gone
So suddenly? She seems in great distress.
And this vow of silence – at a guess
It bodes some terrible catastrophe.

OEDIPUS: Let what must happen happen. But for me
It's vital, humble though they may well be,
To know my origins. Women are allowed
Their share of pride, and yes, Jocasta's proud,
Which makes her jib at my low birth. But I
Am fortune's child – *good* fortune's – which is why
I won't be shamed. Yes, she's my mother. Low
And High – I'm both – and who have made me so?
The Years – my brothers. That's my pedigree.
I shall be true to it. The mystery

Of *my* birth *will* be solved – it has to be.

CHORUS 4:   If I'm not a fool. If I foresee
The future clearly, very soon,
By tomorrow's full moon,
Mount Cithaeron, you are going to be
Exalted. Everyone will honour you
As Oedipus's sister, nurse, and mother too.
We'll celebrate you in our songs and dances, since
You showed such kindness to our prince.
Apollo, tell us what's to come. We call on you:
We're asking you to make our wish come true.

Some nymph was visited by Pan, my son;
It was that mountain wanderer
Who fathered you on her.
Was a bride of Apollo the one
Who bore you? (*He* frequents the mountains too.)
Otherwise, maybe one of Hermes' gave us you?
Bacchus likes the mountains though – was this the scene:
He holds the blessing that has been
Presented to him by a nymph of Helicon –
The kind he's sired so many children on?

OEDIPUS: Well, I never met him. Nonetheless
I think I see our shepherd. That's my guess.
He's old – about *this* fellow's age. What's more
Servants of mine are bringing him. *(to Chorus) You* saw
This person, didn't you?

CHORUS: I know him, yes.
A shepherd known for his trustworthiness.
He was in Laius' service.

Enter Shepherd and Attendants.

OEDIPUS: *(to Messenger)* He's the man?
You can confirm that, I presume?

MESSENGER: I can.

OEDIPUS: You – old man, come here. Look me in the eye.
             Answer my questions, please. In days gone by
             Did you belong to Laius?

SHEPHERD: Born and bred
             In Laius' house, I was – a slave.

OEDIPUS: You led
             What sort of life? What work did you do there?

SHEPHERD: Most of my life I've been a shepherd.

OEDIPUS: Where?

SHEPHERD: On Mount Cithaeron.

OEDIPUS: Where you surely knew
             This fellow here – at least you met him?

SHEPHERD: Who?
             Doing what?

OEDIPUS: This man here. *Have* you met?

SHEPHERD: Sir, I suppose I might have. I forget.

MESSENGER: I'm not surprised he doesn't know me yet.
             But I can quickly jog his memory.
             We were around Cithaeron – him and me.
             He knows. He'd two flocks to *my* one. *(to Shepherd)* Remember?
             (to Oedipus) Six months each year from March until September
             This was – for three years. When the winter came
             I drove my flocks away – he did the same:
             Mine down to *my* fold, his to Laius's. *(to Shepherd)* So:
             Is this the truth I'm telling? Yes or no?

SHEPHERD: All right, it is. But it was years ago.

MESSENGER: You handed me a child. Remember that?
             To bring up as my own?

SHEPHERD: Perhaps? So what?

MESSENGER: This is him.

SHEPHERD: *(makes to strike the Messenger)*
                         Wretch! I've had enough of this.

OEDIPUS: What right have you to chide him? The truth is,
            Your words are reprehensible, not his.

SHEPHERD: Your majesty, you're angry with me – why?

OEDIPUS: He asked about the child – you don't reply.

SHEPHERD: The man's a fool – he's talking nonsense.

OEDIPUS: Well,
            If I must torture you to make you tell
            I shall.

SHEPHERD: I'm old. You mustn't torture me!

OEDIPUS: Quickly – grab his arms, please, somebody.

SHEPHERD: What have I done? What do you want to know?

OEDIPUS: He asked about a baby. Is it so?
            Did you pass it on to him? Well?

SHEPHERD: *Yes!*
            I wish I'd died the day I did.

OEDIPUS: Unless
            You tell the truth, you *will* die.

SHEPHERD: It'll spell
            Certain death – *more* certain – if I tell.

OEDIPUS: He'll play for time, it seems.

SHEPHERD: Play for time? Why, .

I said I gave it to him, didn't I?

OEDIPUS: Where were you given it yourself? Who by?
Or was it yours?

SHEPHERD: No. Someone gave it me.

OEDIPUS: Someone here in Thebes? And who was *he*?
Where did he live?

SHEPHERD: Please – ask me nothing more.

OEDIPUS: Make me ask *again* and you're done for.

SHEPHERD: ... Someone... who lived in Laius's house.

OEDIPUS: I see.
A slave? A member of his family?

SHEPHERD: I'm about to speak the fatal word.

OEDIPUS: And I to hear it, yet it must be heard.

SHEPHERD: Laius. The child was Laius's son, or so
The story went. But ask your wife – she'll know.

OEDIPUS: She gave it you?

SHEPHERD: She did, sire, yes.

OEDIPUS: Why, though?

SHEPHERD: She said I was to kill it.

OEDIPUS: Her own son?
Miserable woman! How could she have done?

SHEPHERD: The prophesies had frightened her?

OEDIPUS: They had?
What prophesies?

SHEPHERD: Well – people said the lad
                   Was one day going to kill his father.

OEDIPUS: Oh?
                   Why give him to this man, if that was so.

SHEPHERD: Because I'd taken pity on him, and
                   I thought *he'd* take him to a foreign land
                   Where he himself had come from. As it was
                   He saved the boy for something worse, because
                   If you're the man he makes you out to be
                   Few lives have turned out so unluckily.

OEDIPUS: The oracles were true! Oh, let my sight
                   Now be replaced by an eternal night,
                   Since horror – only horror's my birthright.
                   It has been shown that I am my wife's son,
                   And killed the one man I should not have done.

CHORUS 5:   The generations come and go.
                   Shadows are what we are – not men.
                   No man is truly happy – none.
                   We only dream we're happy – then,
                   Almost at once the dream is gone.
                   I say that; this is how I know:
                   Your lot, poor Oedipus – is one
                   That makes *mankind's* plain to me:
                   We're all of us born to misery.

                   You hit the mark – won wealth and power.
                   In fact aimed *too* high, possibly,
                   And paid. The sphinx with crooked claws,
                   Who sang her riddle – wasn't she
                   Destroyed by *you*? Since when, of course –
                   Since standing for us like a tower
                   Against death, honours have been yours –
                   High honours. You are king here, and
                   You rule a great and glorious land.

                   They'll weep to hear his story now.
                   Who is more wretched? Look at how

His luck has changed – at how his life
Has been destroyed. Illustrious,
Now most unhappy Oedipus,
Your mother proved to be your wife –
You sowed in soil first sown in by
Your father, yet it did not cry
In horror as you did so – why?

Judging the marriage that was none –
In which the husband was the son –
All-seeing time accuses *you*:
You've sealed your fate unwittingly.
Now my grief pours out of me
In one long cry. Oh, how I rue
The day we met. This much is true:
You gave me back my life – but then
You took the gift away again!

Enter Second Messenger, from the house.

MESSENGER 2: Elders of Thebes, what you're about to hear,
What you'll *witness* presently, will sear
Your hearts with grief. At any rate, if you're still
Loyal to the house of Labdacus it will.
Can any *river* cleanse this palace? How?
A nightmare is concealed inside it now,
Some of which you are about to see –
One that was *sought* – and a catastrophe
We cause is twice as terrible.

CHORUS: We've been
        Crushed by the suffering we've already seen.
        What more is there to tell?

MESSENGER 2:   It's simply said:
        Jocasta, our noble queen, is dead.

CHORUS: Unhappy woman – how? How did she go?

MESSENGER 2: She killed herself. You didn't see, and so
        You're spared the pain of this – at any rate

The worst of it. However, I'll relate
What I recall of that poor creature's fate.
She was in a frenzy of despair.
She rushed into the hallway, and from there
Made for the marriage bed, tearing out her hair
In fistfuls. In the bedroom, first of all
She slammed the doors shut; then began to call
On Laius, long since dead, remembering
Their coupling, long ago, that was to bring
Death to her husband, she being left behind
To bear more children of a monstrous kind;
Wishing she'd had *no* husband, since by one
She'd had another; and to him – her son –
Borne children. How she died I couldn't say:
The king now burst in, screaming – we could pay
No more attention to her – Oedipus
Transfixed us – dashed about – asked each of us
For a sword, and where his wife might be.
"Wife!" he cried. "What sort of wife is she?
She bore my daughters, and my sons, and *me*!"
Who told him where to go? Nobody there.
Some divine force or other showed him where
Jocasta was and, with a ghastly cry,
Just as though he *was* being guided by
Something or someone, he then made a rush
At the double doors; began to push
The bolts that held them, which he wrenched and bent
Out of their sockets, and then in he went –
Or rather fell. She hung there – we all saw –
Dangling from a rope. A terrible roar
Came out him, poor wretch, at this sight. Then
He undid the knot, the noose, and when
The hapless queen was lying on the floor
A worse sight followed: from her dress he tore
The golden brooch that decked it – raised it high
And gouged out first one, then the other eye,
Saying: "Eyes, you mustn't see the wrong
That I have done and suffered. For too long
You've looked on those I wish you'd never seen,
Not recognising those who might have been
So dear to me. You'll see mere darkness, then."

With this, not once but time and time again
He raised the brooch and spiked his eyes. Eyes? No
They were two holes that bled, and with each blow
Spattered his cheeks with blood. The blood came, though,
Not drop by drop but in a shower like rain.
All this appalling suffering, all this pain
Sprang from what both of them themselves had done;
And crushed them – mother-wife and husband-son.
It was true happiness they'd had before.
So long ago that seems now. *This* day saw
Suffering, disaster, death and shame –
Yes, every evil worthy of the name.

CHORUS: Poor Oedipus. His anguish – it's died down?

MESSENGER 2: "Open the gates!" he's shouting. "Show the town
The parricide, the..." No – the word's profane.
He's set on exile – says he won't remain
At home – brave his own curse. He needs someone.
He's weak. He couldn't bear the pain alone.
He'll show you now. They're opening the gates.
I tell you, even somebody who hates
The man would *pity* him. How *couldn't* he,
If he saw what you're about to see?

CHORUS: Terrible sight!
More terrible than anything I ever saw.
What is this madness, wretched man? What divine enemy
Has sent you misery
Such as no one ever knew before?
I can't endure this spectacle, although
There's so much I'd like to ask – so much I want to know:
My horror's *too* great.

OEDIPUS: Pity Oedipus
Where am I going, wretched man? Where do my words go? Where?
They're borne aloft before me on the air.
But, oh, to find my fortunes altered thus!

CHORUS: To learn of this – to witness it – has harrowed us.

OEDIPUS: Engulfed in darkness! In the blackest night!
My anguish is too great – too strong to fight –
Despair! Despair! And pain that stabs right through me –
Just the thought of what has happened to me
Stabs me too.

CHORUS: Lament, as well you might:
You've suffered so much – you *must* cry out then
On your misfortune, and cry out again.

OEDIPUS: Loyal companions; constant friends;
You're kind
You still care for me, although I'm blind.
I *hear* your presence, if I have no eyes
To see with. Could I fail to recognise
Your voices?

CHORUS: What you've done, though, makes no sense.
How? How could you bring yourself to do it?
To put your eyes out! Which god drove you to it?

OEDIPUS: Phobus, it was, and only he, that brought all this about –
Heaped on my head
This woe. But *my* hand, no one else's, dashed my poor eyes out.
What was there I could ever wish to see?
No sight on earth held any joy for me.

CHORUS: There's only too much truth in what you've said.

OEDIPUS: Now nothing could delight my eye – of that I'm in no doubt;
No greeting please my ear.
You must take me far from here.
Get me away immediately. Immediately, I say
I have been destroyed. Indeed, today
There's no one living whom the gods so hate.

CHORUS: Wretched man! You're wretched in your fate
And also in your mind. Oh, how
I wish I'd never known you now!

OEDIPUS: I wish him dead – the man who took those cruel spikes away

And freed me. Yes,
He saved my life. Why should I thank him? Had I died that day
I'd not have been, not to my friends or me,
The burden that, from now on, I must be.

CHORUS: In your place I'd have wished no less.

OEDIPUS: I wouldn't then have killed my father. Nor would people say
My mother was my wife
Mine is a god-forsaken life.
This offspring of unspeakable parents was to get a yield
Of children sown in his own father's field!
Every sorrow known to man, and more,
Oedipus was destined for.

CHORUS: Yet this was madness, to my mind:
Better dead than alive and blind.

OEDIPUS: I know that what I did was for the best:
Don't tell me that it wasn't, or suggest
Some prudent course of action – please – not now.
Had I my sight in Hades, tell me how
I could have borne to see them both again –
My father and my poor, poor mother, when
The wrongs I've done them are of this degree?
Strangling's too light a punishment for me.
Likewise, how could I have wished to see
My *children*, now their parentage is known.
I couldn't; or to set eyes on this town –
The turreted walls, temples and images
Of all the gods? No, such my sad fate is:
I had the best of it in Thebes, and I
Have doomed *myself* to bid it all goodbye.
I ordered you to drive the man away –
The unclean one, whom Phoebus has today
Revealed to be unholy and, what's more,
Laius' son. I'm branded now. Therefore
Could I, from now on,
Look with a steady eye at anyone
In Thebes. Of course not. If there was a way
I'd stop my ears up, too – without delay –

Keep my poor body closed to sight and sound.
Pain might end thus, and some peace be found.

Cithaeron! Why? Why did you shelter me?
Why, rather, did you not immediately
Destroy me – on the day I came to you?
I wouldn't then have shown the whole world who
My parents really were. Oh, Polybus!
Corinth! – ancestral home of Oedipus –
Or so they said you were – you nurtured me –
A lovely thing I was, or seemed to be:
I festered underneath. Now all can see
I'm evil like my parents. Glade and wood –
Three narrowing roads that met and then drank blood –
Mine – that is, my father's, spilled by me –
Have you kept it in your memory –
What you saw me do that day? Also
What I did later, when I came here? Oh,
Sons, fathers, brothers!
Incestuous confusion! Mothers,
Wives! The worst travesties known to men –
Quick, then –
Toss me into the sea,
Where you'll never again set eyes on me.
Come: touch the untouchable. Have no fear.
Do it. There's no one here
But me on whom *this* plague can light.

CHORUS: Creon. In good time. He'll decide what's right –
            Consider your requests – act on them too,
            Since he's ruling now instead of you.

OEDIPUS: What shall I say to him? Considering how
            I've wronged the man, why should he hear me now?

            Enter Creon and Attendants.

CREON: Well, Oedipus, I mustn't mock you, or
            Take you to task for what you did before –
            Wronged though I was by you.
            (to Attendants)   If anyone

Commands your reverence and respect, the Sun –
That god whose warmth gives nourishment to men
Should do so: take this man inside again –
That *must* be Phoebus' will. Spare Thebes the sight
Of a pollution neither earth nor light
Can bear to look on – nor the holy rain.
Into the house with him – at once. His pain
Is something no one in the world but we
His family – and we alone – should see
Or hear. Anything else would not be right.

OEDIPUS: You're a good man. For the gods' love, since, despite
My worthlessness, you seem so strangely kind,
Grant me one favour – something that you'll find
Will prove to yours, and not *my* benefit.

CREON: You want something from me? What is it?

OEDIPUS: Banish me now – don't wait – to where no one
Can ever speak to me.

CREON: I would have done –
Only I wanted first of all to know
What I had to do, from Apollo.

OEDIPUS: Wasn't Apollo's order very plain?
Didn't he tell us to expunge the stain?
Expel the parricide?

CREON: We *were* told so –
In the pass we've now arrived at, though,
It's best to *find out* what to do.

OEDIPUS: I see:
You'd ask the god about a wretch like me?

CREON: Yes. You'll *believe* him this time, *too*, I trust.

OEDIPUS: I shall. You will, I hope – in fact you must –
Give my... Give *her* the burial that *you*
Would hope to have yourself – that must be due

From a brother to his sister. As for me –
Let this, my father's city, never be
Condemned to have me living in it. No,
I wish to live (I hope you'll have it so)
Among the mountains – on Cithaeron – on
The mountain now called mine. It *was* the one
On which my parents wanted me to die
When they were alive. I would thereby
End my life where *they* intended to.
Anyway, I know this much is true:
No common accident or malady
Is ever going to be the end of me.
No, if I was saved from death before
It was certainly for something more
Terrible. But enough of my own fate.
Touching my children: two, at any rate,
Are men now – therefore, Creon, you need give
No thought to them. They'll find the means to live
No matter where they are. My poor girls, though –
They've shared with me in everything. You know,
They've eaten every single meal with me.
Will you please look after them? Maybe
You'll let me touch them now, and grieve.
Sire; noble king; I would believe
I had them, as when I could see,
If I could touch them. Can it be...?

Creon's Attendants lead Antigone and Ismene on.

Is it my girls I hear? Weeping?
Creon took pity on me – had them bring
My two favourite children out to me.
Well? *Has* he?

CREON: Yes, Oedipus, I have – because I knew
How they've always been a joy to you,
Are *now*.

OEDIPUS: Then blessings on you! And for this
May the gods be kind and crown your days with bliss
Great as the grief they've heaped on me today.

Come, daughters – sisters, too – come, let me lay
My hands on you – those hands that, as you see,
Have robbed my eyes of radiance.
(to Antigone and Ismene)   Come to me!
Where are you? Blind I am and blind I was:
Your mother was *my*... I must weep, because
The life that you'll be leading from now on
Is bound to be a sad and bitter one:
The world will see to that. Each gathering,
Each festival that *you* attend will bring
Not joy – there'll be no laughter for you then –
You'll be in tears returning home again.
And when you're old enough to marry, who
Will risk incurring the disgrace that you,
As *my* children – in your own right too –
Would bring with you. What evil's missing, when
Your father killed his father first, and then
Gave his own mother daughters – *you*. They'll fling
Those taunts at you. Who'll think of marrying
You, children? No one. You're condemned, for good.
Of course you are, to sterile spinsterhood.
Son of Menoeceus, all they have is you.
You're their father now. We're gone – we two –
Their natural parents. You must not, therefore,
Leave them to wander – waifs; unmarried; poor.
Remember, they're your flesh and blood and so
You must not ever let them sink as low
As I have sunk, but pity their distress:
You see them – *so* young – *so* alone – unless
You tend them. Will you? Touch me. That means yes.
(to Children) Had you the wisdom that experience brings,
Children, I'd find a hundred helpful things
To say to you. Instead, make this your prayer:
To live where chance allows you to, and there
At least avoid *my* portion of despair.

CREON: Enough lamenting. Go inside now.

OEDIPUS: Well, I must obey,
          Loath though I am.

CREON: All things in season. That's the wisest way

OEDIPUS: First of all you have to grant me...

CREON: *Have* to grant you what?

OEDIPUS: Send me away from here.

CREON: Only the gods can grant you that.

OEDIPUS: But the gods abominate me.

CREON: If that's really so
You'll soon have your wish.

OEDIPUS: You're not deceiving me?

CREON: Oh, no.
What I say I always mean.

OEDIPUS: Take me in.

CREON: Come with us.
Let your children go.

OEDIPUS: Don't take them from me.

CREON: Oedipus,
Please, you mustn't want to have your way in everything.
Not now: your power is won and lost, and you're no longer king.

CHORUS: People of Thebes – look! There goes Oedipus! Yes, it was he
That solved the famous riddle, winning power and majesty.
Everyone envied him his luck. But now a stormy sea
Of terrible misfortune has engulfed him. While we wait
To see the day that *ends* our days, we none of us can state
That we're happy – not we mortals – not until we gain
The boundary where our lives must close, and cross it,
        free of pain.

OEDIPUS AT COLONUS

Cast List

OEDIPUS AT COLONUS recieved its British première in this version at the Royal National Theatre in September 1996. The cast was as follows:

OEDIPUS	ALAN HOWARD
ANTIGONE	TANYA MOODIE
AN ELDER OF COLONUS	HELEN BOURNE
ISMENE	CLARE SWINBURNE
THESEUS	CHRISTIAN BURGESS
CREON	PIP DONAGHY
POLYNEICES	GREG HICKS
MESSENGER	SUZANNE BERTISH
CHORUS/GROUP	JOHN BAXTER, JEAN-BENOIT BLANC, CHRISTOPHER CAMPBELL, MICHAEL CARTER, TAMSIN DIVES, PETER GORDON, SOPHIE GRIMMER, COLIN HURLEY, JEFFERY KISSOON, KATHLEEN MCGOLDRICK, SIMON SCOTT, GRAHAM SINCLAIR, JENNIE STOLLER

DIRECTOR	PETER HALL
DESIGNER	DIONYSIS FOTOPOULOS
LIGHTING	MARK HENDERSON
MUSIC	JUDITH WEIR

OEDIPUS AT COLONUS

The scene is the sacred grove of the Eumenides at Colonus.

OEDIPUS: What country's this, Antigone? Will it give
The wandering Oedipus the means to live?
My wants, if met, are always *barely* met.
I must be satisfied with what I get
Suffering, time, my own nobility
Teach me contentment. Now then, if you see
Some place for me to sit, whether it be
On holy ground, or else on ordinary,
Put me there. Then we'll find out where we are.

ANTIGONE: Father, the city walls – they seem quite far
From here. It's holy ground, this, I should say –
Judging from the fact that vines, and bay
And olive trees are growing all around.
A sacred grove – and full of the sweet sound
Of nightingales. But now, for sitting on,
This rock will serve. Come, rest. You're old.
You've gone quite far enough.

He sits on a rock.

OEDIPUS: Where *are* we?

ANTIGONE: I don't know.
I'm certain that the city's Athens, though.
I'll find out what *this* place is, shall I?

OEDIPUS: Do.

ANTIGONE: There again, perhaps there's no need to:
I can see someone coming.

OEDIPUS: Coming here?
To *us*?

ANTIGONE: He's here. Speak.

OEDIPUS: Sir, we've no idea...

ELDER: I must warn you you're on Holy ground
                You'd better ask your questions when you've found
                A lawful place to...

OEDIPUS: Holy ground, you say?
                Sacred to which god?

ELDER: We all keep away.
                Three great goddesses we're taught to fear –
                Daughters of Earth and Night – their home is here.

OEDIPUS: Indeed? Then I'll invoke them. Their names, please.

ELDER: *Our* name for them is "The Eumenides".

OEDIPUS: I call upon these goddesses to receive
                Their suppliant kindly. I shall never leave
                My chosen refuge.

ELDER: Please explain to me...

OEDIPUS: This is a sign. It means my destiny.

ELDER: I daren't myself force you to leave this spot:
                Without the town's permission I cannot.
                I'll go and say you're sitting here.

OEDIPUS: First, though,
                Before you leave – there's something I must know;
                This is a sacred place, but where *are* we?

ELDER: Here's what I know: in its entirety
                This place is sacred to Poseidon – he
                In all his greatness, guards it. Then again
                A titan – one who first brought fire to men –
                Prometheus – has his place here too. You stand
                Upon the "Brazen threshold" of this land.
                For so it's called. The local people claim
                A hero as their founder, and his name

The place now bears: Colonus.

OEDIPUS:
                                        Governing
Colonus there's a council – or a king...

ELDER: The Athenian king – Aegëus' son.

OEDIPUS: Well, a great favour for a little one
Is what I'm offering. Send for him.

ELDER:
                                        What *kind*
Of service can you do him? Why, you're blind.

OEDIPUS: Wait till he's heard.

ELDER:
                        I want you safe, my friend:
Wretched you may be, but in the end
Nobility's what counts. To look at *you*
I'd say you were noble through and through.
Wait here, then, where I found you, while I go
And let the people of Colonus know
What's passed between us. They will then decide
Whether you should be granted or denied
A refuge here.

The Elder goes. Oedipus kneels in prayer.

OEDIPUS:
                        Great goddesses, smile on me –
And on Apollo also: it was he
Who, in the very oracle which said
That evils would be heaped upon my head,
Also assured me that I *would* find rest –
On coming to the object of my quest –
A country where I'd find a place like this –
Sacred to three feared goddesses, that is –
My refuge. There my life would reach its close,
He told me – suffering cease at last. To those
Who harboured me, my sojourn here would bring
Great benefits – a bitter reckoning
To those who drove me from my home. What's more
He told me of a sign – an earthquake, or

Thunder, or lightning. Now I feel some force
That came from you three set me on my course
Here, to this sacred grove of yours. If not,
Why, in my wanderings, would I choose this spot
Before all others? Why have settled here –
On rough but holy ground? I am austere –
Sobriety itself; you're sober too –
Offerings of wine are never made to you.
Fulfill Apollo's prophesy, which was clear:
That when my race was run I'd end it here.
That's if you don't despise me – I whose woes
Are worse than any other mortal knows.
Dear daughters of primeval darkness, hear!
City of Pallas, Athens, lend an ear!
Most glorious of all cities, pity me!
Pity the poor wraith, Oedipus! You see
A broken man before you.

Enter Chorus.

CHORUS: Who is he?
Where is he?
Where is he hiding them?
This most impudent of men?
He's a stranger – he must be:
He's trespassed in their sacred grove.
The Goddesses we dread above
All others – dare not name
But pass with eyes averted. This man came
And where we show such reverence, showed none!
Where is he? Where's he gone?

Oedipus and Antigone step forward.

OEDIPUS: I'm here and as they say
My ears are my eyes. I can't find my way
Without this girl to guide me.

CHORUS: *(to Oedipus)*   Were you born blind? I'd have said
You've had long years of suffering
To look at you. I know one thing:

I'm not about to let you bring a curse down on your head
For trespassing here. You've gone
Where you should not have. There's a glade –
Keep silent – where mixed offerings are made –
Water and honey – don't go on!
Unhappy stranger, please beware,
Don't enter there!
You want to speak to us? First quit
Ground that nobody's allowed to tread
And come and talk with us instead
Where sacred laws have sanctioned it.

OEDIPUS: Child, I'll act as you advise me to.

ANTIGONE: Let's do what they would have us do.

OEDIPUS: Then take my hand.

CHORUS: This is your refuge now. No one
            Will ever make you leave it.

OEDIPUS: Have I gone
            Far enough?

CHORUS: Further still.

ANTIGONE: *(to Oedipus)*   Come – this way.

CHORUS: You must now revere
            What is revered by Athens – and what *she* fears *you* must fear.

OEDIPUS: Lead me, child, to where
            Their sacred laws allow it – there
            We'll speak to them. So it must be.
            Let us accept necessity.

CHORUS: Don't go beyond that ledge.

OEDIPUS: This far?

CHORUS: Stop just where you are.

Antigone sits Oedipus down on the ledge.

CHORUS: Who are you and where from?

OEDIPUS: I am an exile. But...

CHORUS: But what?

OEDIPUS: Don't ask me who I am. Don't pry.

CHORUS: Why not?

OEDIPUS: My birth was monstrous.

CHORUS: Yes? Go on...

OEDIPUS: Child – what shall I say?

CHORUS: Who was your father? Speak!

ANTIGONE: *(to Oedipus)*   You've all but told them anyway...

OEDIPUS: Yes – I'll confess it.

CHORUS: Do! Now!

OEDIPUS: Laius' son –

CHORUS: No...!

OEDIPUS: The house of Labdacus...

CHORUS: Oh, Zeus!

OEDIPUS: The hapless Oedipus –
You've heard of them?

CHORUS: Are you that man, then?

OEDIPUS: Don't be frightened.

The Chorus shrink from him in horror.

CHORUS: Go!
          Leave Colonus!

OEDIPUS: Aren't you going to keep your promise?

CHORUS: No.
          And the gods won't punish us: we're playing false with *you*
          But *you* played false with us.

ANTIGONE: If what he did – and never knew
          What he was doing – makes you spurn my father, pity *me*:
          I supplicate you for *his* sake – this man of misery –
          I supplicate you as a daughter might
          A father and, with eyes still blessed with sight,
          Look into yours: oh, let him meet
          With your compassion. Our dependence on you is complete.
          You are like gods to us. Come then, be kind.
          Show us the sympathy we dared not hope to find.
          Grant it, by all you hold most dear in life –
          By wealth, by gods, by children and by wife.
          Show me the man who, once a god had led him on,
          Could escape ruin. Scour the world and you will not find one.

CHORUS: Daughter of Oedipus, we pity you
          For your bad fortune – and your father too –
          But we're afraid of what the gods may do
          If we say more.

OEDIPUS: And what good ever came
          Of good repute not earned; of hollow fame?
          I'd heard that Athens held the gods in awe.
          "If a safe haven's what you're looking for
          And assistance, too, that's where you go,"
          They say. For me, at least, it isn't so:
          You're forcing me to leave. My name alone
          Has frightened you – not me, or what I've done.
          Done? No – that's not the word. I suffered rather
          Than acted, if my mother and my father
          Have to be spoken of. Yes – *they're* the cause

Of this alarm – this panic fear of yours.
How am I a bad man? I was hit –
I hit back. Why, even for doing it
With *knowledge,* I would not have been to blame.
As it was I... came where I came,
Knowing *nothing.* Take me in. My face
Is hideous, but I'm in a state of grace –
Holy. Don't spurn me. You all stand to gain
By my presence here, as I'll explain
When the king comes. Meanwhile, be kind to me.

CHORUS: We'll let the king decide this.

OEDIPUS: Where is he?

CHORUS: We've sent for him.

ANTIGONE: Oh, Zeus! What shall I say
Or think? Father...

OEDIPUS: What, child?

ANTIGONE: Coming this way –
A girl on horseback. It's your daughter, sir –
Ismene. When she speaks you'll know it's her.

Ismene enters, accompanied by a servant.

ISMENE: Dear sister! Dearest father! High and low
I've *hunted* for you; here you are, and now
It's just as hard to look at you – to see
A sight so painful.

OEDIPUS: Can it really be...?

ISMENE: Oh, poor father – a heart rending sight!

OEDIPUS: You came.

ISMENE: So many obstacles. Despite
Them all, I came.

OEDIPUS: Then touch me.

ISMENE: And her too.

She holds out a hand to each.

OEDIPUS: Daughters! Sisters!

ISMENE: How you suffer, both of you.

OEDIPUS: We suffer?

ISMENE: Yes, you suffer – as I do.

OEDIPUS: What brought you?

ISMENE: Love. I've news, too.

OEDIPUS: Won't *they* play
            Their part as well – your brothers? Where are *they*
            To assist me?

ISMENE: They are where they are –
            In danger, too.

OEDIPUS: I put them on a par
            With men of Egypt, where the wives, it's said,
            Go out into the world to win the bread,
            While husbands sit at home and weave. Likewise,
            Who bear my load, while those with whom it lies
            To do so, girl-like, stay at home? You two!
            You help this poor wretch, *not* them. Since she grew
            Into a strong young woman, one of you
            Has been an old man's guide – always the one
            With me, wandering through wild woods – woe-begone,
            Barefoot and hungry and drenched to the bone
            By rain; burned by the sun – but this distress
            Was nothing to her. Nothing mattered less
            To *her* than her own ease, and nothing more
            Than mine. And you, child, brought me word, before,
            Of any oracles that were about

My destiny; then, when I was cast out
Stood loyally by me. So you've news today?
What is it? Something terrible, I dare say.

ISMENE: Your sons now face disaster. Glad at first
(Both feeling that their family was cursed)
To leave the crown with Creon, and so spare
Thebes the miasma which they were aware
Hung over your ill-fated house, and had
Time out of mind – now they have both gone mad.
Some god is goading them: they're battling
For power – they're both determined to be king.
The younger's robbed the elder of his throne –
Driven him from Thebes. An exile, he has gone,
We're told, to Argos – found a new ally
And men who'll fight with him. He means, thereby,
Either to triumph – conquer Thebes – or die.
And then there are the oracles.

OEDIPUS: What are they?
            Child, what's been prophesied?

ISMENE: This: that one day
            Thebes will have need of you, alive and dead –
            Your presence there will stand her in good stead.

OEDIPUS: And how could I help anyone?

ISMENE: It's said
            Her power will rest with you.

OEDIPUS: I'm someone, then,
            Now that I'm no one.

ISMENE: Yes, for once again
            The gods are with you.

OEDIPUS: With me when my time
            Is over! They destroyed me in my prime.

ISMENE: Soon – very soon – Creon will come to you

Because the gods are with you.

OEDIPUS: What to do?

ISMENE: To place you *near* Thebes – in her power – and yet
Beyond her borders.

OEDIPUS: Oh? What will they get
From me not *inside* Thebes? What benefit?

ISMENE: If something untoward happens to it
Your tomb will hold a curse for them.

OEDIPUS: It will.
No need for oracles to tell us.

ISMENE: Still,
That's why they want you near Thebes. Then, you see,
You'd be their tool.

OEDIPUS: And will they bury me
In Theban soil at any rate?

ISMENE: They can't
Because you killed your father.

OEDIPUS: Then they shan't –
Even for one day – have charge of me.

ISMENE: That will cost them dear eventually.

OEDIPUS: How?

ISMENE: Your wrath, when they confront your tomb.

OEDIPUS: And what you've told me, child, you heard from whom?

ISMENE: Men who brought oracles from Delphi.

OEDIPUS: So:
Apollo said *this* of me! My sons know?

ISMENE: Yes.

OEDIPUS: They didn't want me with them, though.
               Being evil, they preferred the crown.
               May the gods prevent its dying down –
               Their conflict let it rage on. And what's more
               May *I* be arbitrator in the war
               They're now engaged in: if I were, the one
               Who has them now would not retain his throne
               And sceptre, while the exiled one would stay
               In exile. I was being driven away
               Shamefully from my country – and did *they*
               Take steps to stop it, or defend me? No.
               They looked on – saw their father forced to go –
               Thrust out of house and home – they listened while
               He was proclaimed, in public, an exile,
               And failed to act. I wanted it, you'll say –
               Was given what I'd asked for anyway –
               And that was right. Not so. On the first day,
               When I was mad and death seemed sweet to me –
               Yes, even death by stoning – nobody
               Was ready to oblige me. Later on,
               When anguish, or the worst of it, had gone,
               When my own self-loathing had begun
               To seem to me too great for what I'd done –
               The price I'd paid myself too high; and when
               So many months had passed, why it was then
               That I was hounded out of Thebes. One word
               From *my sons* would have stopped this – was it heard?
               Oh, no. They could have helped, but both failed me.
               They left me to a life of vagrancy
               And never-ending exile. From these two –
               Girls, mark you – I receive the service due
               From family: shelter, food. My sons would rather
               Gain power a kingdom – than *re*gain a father.
               I'll not be either's ally – no, not I.
               And neither son will ever profit by
               Becoming king of Thebes. That much I know.
               The oracle she speaks of proves it so –
               Supports the one given me long ago,
               Which Phoebus has accomplished finally.

Let Creon, then, be sent in search of me –
Or anyone with power in Thebes. For, friends,
If you're prepared to act in my defence,
Assisted by your native goddesses,
Whom all dread, then the certain outcome is:
Disaster for my enemies, and for *you* –
For Athens – a great saviour.

CHORUS: Friend, we do –
Indeed, *must* – pity you, and your daughters too.
And since you add a promise to your plea –
A promise to preserve us, take from me
A piece of sound advice.

OEDIPUS: Please give it, friend.
Give it in kindness and you can depend
On my obedience.

CHORUS: Then I counsel you
To offer such libations as are due
The powers whose ground you trespassed on just now.

OEDIPUS: Propitiate the goddesses? But how?

CHORUS: You must fetch a sacred offering
Of water, drawn from a perennial spring.
Take your bowls; put lambswool, freshly shorn –
Festoons of it – round each. Turn to the dawn
And pour three times – with honeyed water, not
One drop of wine.

OEDIPUS: When, in some shady spot,
The earth has drunk my offerings...?

CHORUS: Then lay there
Some olive sprays, with both hands and this prayer:
That, as we call them kind, these goddesses,
So they'll receive a suppliant, who *is*
Our shield, with kindness. When you speak it, too –
You, or someone sent to act for you –
Speak low. Then leave. Do this, or else I fear

For *you*, my friend.

OEDIPUS: *(to Antigone and Ismene)* You heard them. They live here.

ISMENE: We heard. What must we do, then?

OEDIPUS: *I* can't go –
I'm weak and blind. Let one of you. I know
That one sincere soul, as a deputy,
Can discharge this duty – yes, for me –
And for ten thousand like me. Don't delay.
I can't walk alone, though – one must stay
To guide me and support me.

ISMENE: Let *me* go.
I'll offer this libation up. *(to Chorus)* Where, though?

CHORUS: In the grove – on the far side from here.
If you need guidance, there's a guardian there
He'll help you.

             Exit Ismene.

                        What you asked for has been done:
They've sent for Theseus, Aegeus' son –
The king. He's here.

THESEUS: Who wouldn't recognise
You, son of Laius, by those wretched eyes.
What has brought you here, a hapless pair –
You and the girl who stands beside you there?
Say what you want. Tell me of horrors. None
I could conceive of now would make me shun,
Or shrink from helping you. For I, of course,
Was raised an exile. *My* lot *was* like *yours*.
I met with dangers in strange countries – more
Than any man had ever faced before:
How could I not help you, then? I know –
Know all too well – that I'm a man, and so,
Even tomorrow, mightn't *my* life be
What yours is now?

OEDIPUS: From those words I can see
                    I need say little. Who I am, and who
                    My father was, you've said – my city, too,
                    You *could* name. Then I'll state my wants.

THESEUS: Do so.

OEDIPUS: I've come to give you my poor body. No,
                    Not an enticing gift – you'll profit, though,
                    From harbouring it here.

THESEUS: And may we know
                    What blessing you have brought?

OEDIPUS: That will be clear
                    Once I'm dead and buried – by you, here.

THESEUS: Then for life's *last* need I can serve your turn –
                    What might preceed it is of no concern
                    To you?

OEDIPUS: That takes in everything I want.

THESEUS: Few requests are easier to grant.

OEDIPUS: Strife will follow.

THESEUS: With your sons, maybe?

OEDIPUS: Yes. For they're intent on forcing me
                    To go back home to Thebes.

THESEUS: But why not go?
                    It's wrong for you to be in exile.

OEDIPUS: No.
                    After all, they wouldn't let me stay
                    When I wanted to.

THESEUS: A foolish way
                    To talk! What earthly use can anger be

In bad times?

OEDIPUS: *Hear* me – *then* find fault with me.

THESEUS: I'll judge when I've learned everything.

OEDIPUS: You see,
In Thebes I suffered wrong – a heinous wrong.

THESEUS: The curse that's dogged your family for so long –
That's what you mean?

OEDIPUS: No. I'll explain my plight.
Driven from my country by my sons, the right
To go back is withheld from me – denied
Because I'm Oedipus the parricide.

THESEUS: You're not to live there? Then I don't see how
They could recall you.

OEDIPUS: But they have to now:
There was an oracle.

THESEUS: What did it say
It frightened them?

OEDIPUS: It said they're doomed, some day,
To meet disaster here.

THESEUS: I see no way
A conflict could arise between your sons
And me.

OEDIPUS: But aren't the gods the only ones
Who don't grow old or die? For here below
What is there that can either live or grow –
Man, beast or plant – that doesn't undergo
Change and decay? Time conquers everything:
Faith fades and soon mistrust is flourishing.
Friends become enemies, then friends again
As the years pass. As easily as men,

Cities fall out. And therefore, though today
You and the Thebans are firm friends, there may –
Will come a time – eventually – when they
Will take up arms against you, and destroy
The concord that you currently enjoy
In some absurd cause. My cold corpse, I say,
Will, though it sleeps beneath the ground, one day
Drink their warm blood – if Apollo spoke true –
If Zeus is still Zeus. What I may not do
Is speak of mysteries. Permit me, then,
To end where I began and ask again
For refuge in your country. Do one thing –
Keep faith – and you'll confess that harbouring
Oedipus in your kingdom was most wise –
Unless, of course, the gods themselves tell lies.

THESEUS: *(to Chorus)* This is a favour we cannot deny:
For one thing he's a Theban – an ally:
We owe him hospitality. And then
There are the gods he supplicated when,
Bringing great *blessings* to this land and me,
He came here. All his claims, accordingly,
Must be respected. I will never spurn
His kindness to us. Since it serves his turn
To stay here, you must make it your concern
To see that he's protected. I intend
To grant him citizenship. But, my friend,
If you would rather come with me, please do.
The choice is yours. In short, I'm granting you
Whatever you desire.

OEDIPUS: Zeus, may such men
Prosper, with Your help.

THESEUS: What's your preference, then?
To come with *me* now?

OEDIPUS: Were it lawful to.
My place is here, though.

THESEUS: And you mean to do

What here, exactly? I won't interfere.

OEDIPUS: I'll destroy the men who drove me here.
But keep your word.

THESEUS: Don't worry – I mean to.

OEDIPUS: I ask for *no* oath, since I know you're true.
Their men will come for me...

THESEUS: And *these* men here
Will deal with them.

OEDIPUS: But look – you've no idea...
Leave me, and...

THESEUS: Are you teaching me my part?

OEDIPUS: How can I help it? I'm afraid.

THESEUS: *My* heart
Can feel no fear.

OEDIPUS: Their threats, though – if you knew...

THESEUS: I know this: nobody is taking you
Without my leave. Oh maybe angry men
Have blustered at me time and time again –
Loud threats they've made, and all were made in vain.
They soon regain their senses, though – and then
Their threats seemed so much breath. You say these men
Have spoken – spoken boldly, it may be,
Of taking you to Thebes. Believe you me
They'd have a hard time of it if they tried.
So have no fears on *that* score. And beside
Any resolve of mine, remember this:
You shouldn't be at *all* afraid: that is
Not if Apollo sent you to us. Still
While I'm not here to shield you my name will.

Theseus exits.

CHORUS: Attica's famous for its horses. There
          The loveliest place on earth is to be found
          And *you* have found it: white Colonus, where
          The clear-voiced nightingale sings all year round –

          Frequents the wine-dark ivy in the shade
          Of Bacchus' secret bower, that must abound
          In fruit of every kind – a leafy glade –
          One into which no sunlight ever found

          Its way; where no wind ever whistled; where
          The god of revels wanders, as he will
          Until time ends. He knew the tender care
          Of nymphs when young – they walk there with him still.

          Narcissi bloom there, watered by the dew
          And thickly-flowered. The two earth-goddesses
          Have always worn them as a crown. There, too,
          The golden crocus flourishes. There is

          A spring that never fails, and from it flow
          The wandering waters of a crystal stream –
          The Cephisus. They cross the plain and so –
          Once touched by them – the fertile earth will teem.

          Now, the nine muses love this place also –
          So, too, does Aphrodite. There's a tree
          The like of which I never heard of – no,
          There's none in Asian soil, nor can there be

          On Pelops' great peninsular – a tree
          That's self-renewing – that has never been
          Destroyed by the invading enemy;
          It grows in *this* land most of all: I mean

          The olive, with its leaves of silver grey.
          It gives our children nourishment, and who
          Will ever harm it? No one: night and day
          Zeus guards it, and grey-eyed Athene too.

          I have another reason, though, to praise

Our great metropolis, given to her by
A mighty god – a gift that served to raise
This country's glory higher than the sky:

The power of unbacked colts and of the sea.
Because, Poseidon, son of Kronos, you
Exalted her – taught her the mastery
Of horses with the curb that can subdue

Their untamed spirit; and the use of oars
Plied easily by men to help them speed
Over the deep – that gift was also yours –
It lets us follow where the sea-nymphs lead.

ANTIGONE: *(to Chorus)* High praise for any country – none *so* high.
Praise it's time for you to justify.

OEDIPUS: What's happening, child?

ANTIGONE: It's Creon and his men –
Coming towards us now.

OEDIPUS: *(to Chorus)*   It *is* time, then,
My friends: you have to prove that I'm safe here.

CHORUS: We shall prove it. What have you to fear?
Old and weak though we ourselves may be,
This state is strong.

                Enter Creon and his Guards.

CREON: My noble friends, I see
That my arrival here has given rise
To some alarm – I read it in your eyes.
Don't shrink from me, or speak unkindly. Why,
I plan to use no force; I'm old, aren't I?
Moreover, I acknowledge that nowhere –
No city in all Greece – can now compare
In power with Athens. No, sirs, I've been sent
(And let me tell you that I represent
Not one man, but my nation) to persuade

This exile to return home. I was made
The envoy, since I felt his misery
Most, as his kinsman. *(to Oedipus)* Come back home with me.
Unhappy Oedipus. You hear our plea:
All Thebes appeals to you, and rightly so –
But I above all, seeing what a blow
The sight of your great suffering is to me –
Outcast that you are, perpetually
Wandering from place to place – a pauper, too –
Unhappy man! And who looks after you?
Only this girl. I never thought that she
Would ever have to live so wretchedly –
Poor creature! Why, she leads a *beggar's* life
And has to tend you always. Someone's *wife*
She ought to be by now. Instead, one day,
A man you come across along the way
Takes her! This shames our family, and us.
Come back to Thebes, I beg you, Oedipus.
By all the gods our forebears worshipped, come!
Consent! Return to your ancestral home.
First take a friendly leave of this great land –
You chose her well, but yours must still command
Your first allegiance.

OEDIPUS: Zeus, you're impudent!
You'll find some super-subtle argument
To tip the scales your way. Again you try
To cause me pain beyond endurance. Why?
Why do you want to trap me? Years ago,
When my own crimes had made me mad, and so
I longed to be an exile from our land,
You stopped me leaving. On the other hand,
When all the turmoil in my mind died down
And it seemed best to stay in my own town,
Then I was ejected – driven away.
Family ties weren't on your mind that day!
Now, when you see this city treating me
With kindness, and her people's courtesy
Towards me, Creon, you attempt to tear me
Away from her. You're seeking to ensnare me
With wheedling words that hide your cruel intent.

Even if your proposal *were* well meant,
Why should I welcome it? What you denied
When it was wanted, now I'm satisfied –
Have shelter here – you'd give me! Generous, no?!
What would *you* call such kindness? Empty show.
Yet you're treating me in just this way,
And your intent is bad, though what you say
Seems good. But let me tell these people, too,
How bad a man you are: what you would do
Is not escort me home – far from it. No –
You want to keep me *outside* Thebes, and so
Ward any threat from Athens off. What's worse
Than failing in your aim is this: my curse
Hanging over Thebes: my sons will win
So much of *my* realm as they're *buried* in.
I think you'll find I have a clearer view –
Far clearer – of the fate of Thebes than you.
For what my sources say is always true:
Apollo first, and Zeus himself – *they* told me:
You'll rue the day you came here and cajoled me
With endless treacherous talk. From which you'll gain,
Believe me, nothing good, but only pain.
But you *won't* believe me. Then just go!
Let us live here. Are we wretched? No.
We can't be, since our lot suffices us.

CREON: Indeed? Who'll suffer most then, Oedipus,
            If this is your position? Me or you?

OEDIPUS: *I'll* be happy if you fail to woo
            My friends – if they contemn your wheedling too.

CREON: Wretched man! So foolish, at this stage
            In life? You bring dishonour on old age.

OEDIPUS: You've a glib tongue – no *good* man known to me
            Could argue, with the same facility,
            A good case or a bad.

CREON: You've said a lot,
            And nonetheless said nothing.

OEDIPUS: Meaning what?
                That *you've* been brief, said all that need be said?

CREON: No, since I'm talking to a dunderhead.

OEDIPUS: Be off with you! I speak for them, too.

                He indicates the Chorus.

                                            Go!
                Don't menace me. I choose to live here.

CREON: So –
                This is your answer? If I take you...

OEDIPUS: How?
                When people with such power support me now?

CREON: You'll have your share of grief in any case.

OEDIPUS: Why do you throw this new threat in my face?

CREON: Because I've seized Ismene. She's been sent
                Back home to Thebes. The other one I'm bent
                On taking shortly.

OEDIPUS: No!

CREON: There's more distress
                In store for you.

OEDIPUS: You've seized Ismene?

CREON: Yes.
                And I intend to take the other one
                In next to no time.

OEDIPUS: Friends, what's to be done?
                Will you forsake me? Won't you drive away
                This godless man?

CHORUS: *(to Creon)*   You! Leave this land! *I* say
            You've done wrong – then and now.

CREON: *(to Guards)*   No more delay.
            Use force if need be, but remove her – now!

ANTIGONE: Where can I run to? Who will help and how?
            What god or man?

CHORUS: *(to Creon)*   You'll sieze her then?

CREON: I vow
            I won't touch Oedipus – Antigone
            I mean to have. She's mine by right.

OEDIPUS: *(to Chorus)*   Help me...!

CHORUS: *(to Creon)* This is wrong.

CREON: I've merely claimed my own.

OEDIPUS: Help! Hear me in the town!

CHORUS: *(to Creon)* What are you doing? Let her go!
            You'll have to fight us soon, my friend.

CREON: Get back, please.

CHORUS: No.
            Not if this is what you now intend.

CREON: I warn you, war with Thebes will be the price of harming me.

OEDIPUS: *(to Chorus)* I told you this would happen.

CHORUS: *(to Creon)*   Let her go immediately!

CREON: Don't give an order that you can't enforce.

CHORUS: Again I say:
            Let the girl go!

CREON: And I say: keep away!

CHORUS: Citizens, come here! A crushing blow
               Is being dealt our city.

ANTIGONE: Help! Help me!

OEDIPUS: Where are you?

ANTIGONE: I've been taken – brutally!

OEDIPUS: Hold out your hands to me.

ANTIGONE: I'm helpless!

CREON: *(to Guards)*   You –
               Take her! Now!

OEDIPUS: Misery! What am I to do?

The Guards go, leading Antigone off with them.

CREON: *(to Oedipus)* That pair were your support, but now they're gone.
               You walk alone and will do from now on.
               But since you *have* to win let's say you've won –
               Beaten your country and your family.
               I know this much: in time you'll come to see
               That now, and in the past, you have done wrong
               By giving in to rage, which, all along,
               Has been your ruin.

CHORUS: *(Grabbing hold of Creon)*   Wait!

CREON: No! Let me go!

CHORUS: You must give him back his daughters.

CREON: No!

CHORUS: We won't release you till you have.

CREON: I fear
                His daughters won't be all I take from here
                You're giving Thebes a greater prize today.

CHORUS: What will you do?

CREON: Take Oedipus away.

CHORUS: Take Oedipus? Well, that would be a blow.
                I doubt if you're equipped to strike it, though.

OEDIPUS: If these fearsome goddesses permit
                A second curse, oh, let me utter it!
                (to Creon) Wretch! You have robbed me of Antigone,
                Through whom, though sightless, I could always see.
                Then let the sun god, who sees all things, send
                To you and yours this fate: may *your* days end
                Like mine.

                    Enter Theseus and two Attendants.

THESEUS: What's this?

OEDIPUS: I know that voice by now –
                Theseus! I've been wronged, and cruelly.

THESEUS: How?
                By whom?

OEDIPUS: Creon – you see him? – took from me
                My two beloved children.

THESEUS: *Why* did he?

OEDIPUS: I told you I'd been wronged and now you know.

THESEUS: *(to Attendants)* Find my people. Tell them they're to go
                Without delay to where the highways meet,
                As fast as horses, or their own two feet
                Can take them. If he gets those girls away
                This fellow will have every right to say

He got the better of me.

An Attendant goes.

(to Creon)   What you've done
Dishonours me, and Thebes, and everyone
From whom you are descended. Entering
A realm where justice, more than anything,
Has been, *will be* upheld – where nobody
Would act unlawfully – you sought to be
Outside the law – swooped down and whisked away,
By *force*, your chosen captives; I dare say
You thought there were no men here, or maybe
Nothing but slaves, and quite discounted *me*.

CREON: You shelter him. Why? I don't understand.
He killed his father; he's polluted; *and*
Those daughters he was with were born him by
A wife who... Foul! Foul!

OEDIPUS: *(to Creon)*   You revile me. Why?
An oracle tells my father he's to die
By his son's hand. Is that *my* fault? No.
I wasn't *born* then. Yes, I *killed* him. So?
How can you blame me, when I never knew
What I did? That is, who I did it *to*?
When you're attacked, what action do you take?
Deal with your attackers, or first make
Enquiries? Ask if one of them's your father?
You – *any* man who loved his life would rather
Ask questions later. Turning to my mother:
We were... doubly tied to one another.
The shame of it! She bore my sons. It's true.
But I plead ignorance in *this* case too.
You seem to have forgotten, furthermore,
That this city holds the gods in awe –
None more so. I'm their suppliant, and *you*
Have done me grievous wrong – have robbed me, too,
Of both my daughters.

CHORUS: *(to Theseus)*   He's a righteous man.

He's been cursed by fate but, if we can,
We ought to help him.

THESEUS: No more talk. While *we*,
Their victims, stand here and are desultory,
The men who wronged us speed away.

CREON: How, though,
Can I assist? I can't. I'm powerless.

THESEUS: No.
You can tell us where your men have gone.

CREON: Once back in Thebes I'll think of...

THESEUS: Threats? Lead on.

Exeunt Theseus, his Attendants and Creon.

CHORUS: I long to be
Where the retreating enemy
Are held at bay –
Are forced to turn, enter the fray –
The brazen clangour of battle, by that shore
Loved by Apollo, or
On that other, torchlit strand
Where the great goddesses demand
Funeral rites
For all their acolytes –
All those on whom their priests have set the seal –
The golden seal of silence. And I feel –
I *know* that, on whichever shore,
Theseus will find the girls who've just been carried off, before
They're out of Attica. Victorious cries will ring out then –
And what's more they'll be raised by Theseus' men.

Or it may be
That in their flight, the enemy
Will reach the far-off country where
The snow-capped mountain are, borne there
By horses and swift chariots. But Creon

Will never win: no one
Can fight as Theseus' followers do.
The force *we've* sent is fearsome too.
The glint of steel
On bridle, as they wheel
And charge at speed, and wheel and charge again!
Every man will give his mount full rein –
Our horsemen, faithful worshippers
Of Pallas, for the art of riding is a gift of hers –
Hers and Poseidon's, whom they worship too – Rea's favourite son.
Are they about to clash? Has it begun?

This much I know:
These girls, who've suffered so –
Their trials will soon end. Zeus
Won't let us lose.

CHORUS: *(to Oedipus)* Well now, my friend, you will not say of me
              That I was a false prophet: I can see
              Your daughters coming. Yes, they're drawing near.

OEDIPUS: What? Where are they?

CHORUS: They're being escorted here
              By...

              Enter Theseus, his Attendants, Antigone and Ismene.

OEDIPUS: Children...?!

ANTIGONE: Theseus rescued us!

OEDIPUS: Come here.
              Let me hold you now. It was my fear
              That you were lost for good.

ANTIGONE: We've longed, like you,
              To hold – be held.

OEDIPUS: Where are you?

ANTIGONE: Here.

Oedipus embraces Antigone and Ismene.

OEDIPUS: You two
            Have been my sole support.

ANTIGONE: Wretched support
            For a wretched man.

OEDIPUS: But with my darlings caught
            In my embrace, I *could* die – wretched, yes –
            But not entirely so. Come children – press
            Close to your father – cling to me, and so
            The ordeals that I've had to undergo
            Can be forgotten. Tell me – briefly, though –
            Brevity's best at your age – how it was.

ANTIGONE: You'd best let Theseus tell you that, because
            He was the one who saved us. Was I brief?

OEDIPUS: *(to Theseus) Since* they've been saved, when it was my belief
            That they were lost, don't marvel if I linger
            In eager talk with them. You are the bringer
            Of this great joy – of my two girls – to me.
            You freed them – no one else. Accordingly
            May the gods deal as I would wish them to
            With you and Athens. Theseus, in my view,
            You're paragons of fairness, honesty
            And piety. These virtues I can see
            So clearly, since I owe you everything.
            You helped me – no one else has. Yes, my king,
            Give me your hand – I want to touch it – please –
            And kiss your cheek... What mad requests are these?
            An abject sinner, tainted through and through,
            Wishes a man so wholly pure as you
            To touch him! Folly! If you *wanted* to
            I wouldn't let you. Those and only those
            Who've shared in them should help me bear my woes.
            So I salute you, but stay where you are –
            Promise you'll help me as you have so far –

Faithfully – in the future.

THESEUS: A report
Has reached me, Oedipus. It calls for thought.
It seems a man – your kinsman, so they say,
Though not from Thebes, is here. He's made his way
Up to Poseidon's shrine – a suppliant.

OEDIPUS: Where has he come from and what does he want?

THESEUS: To talk to you, I'm told.

OEDIPUS: To talk to me?
About what? He's a suppliant is he?
It must be something of importance, then.

THESEUS: He wants to talk and then go home again
In safety.

OEDIPUS: This – this is my loathsome son.
King Theseus, I can't think of anyone
I'm less inclined to listen to.

THESEUS: But why?

OEDIPUS: You won't persuade me and you needn't try.
I *will* not hear him.

THESEUS: He's a suppliant, though –
Aren't you bound? The reverence that you owe
The god – doesn't it...?

ANTIGONE: Let our brother come.
Other men have wicked sons, and some
Have fiery tempers too. They listen, though,
To soft persuasion from their friends, and so
Their mood will mellow. Keep the past in view –
Forget today – recall what you went through –
All owing to your parents. Then you'll see –
I know you will – what misery must be
The fruit of ill-judged anger. Ponder it.

You've more than ample reason to – to wit
Your sightless eyes.

She indicates Theseus.

OEDIPUS: Well, well, my child, you've won.
I'm granting you your wish – the very one
I'm least disposed to grant. *(to Theseus)* Please promise me
Before you send him here that neither he
Nor any other man will ever take
Charge of my life.

THESEUS: Old man, you mustn't make
The same request a second time. Be sure
That while I live and breathe, you are secure.

Exit Theseus.

CHORUS: Oh, the utter folly of the man
Who wants to live beyond a moderate span,
For life is full of incident, far less goes right than wrong,
And there's no joy for those who live too long.
Relief is sure to come at last, when Hades' stern decree
Is issued for us all. And then there'll be
No wedding song or dancing, and no lyre will play.
Death will dominate our final day.

Never to have been born is best by far –
And second best, I'm certain, once we are,
To go back where we came from – quickly, too.
Are you young, care-free, wild? Awaiting you
Just round the corner are afflictions: Envy, faction, strife,
Battles, murder, at the end of life
Old age is there – unloved, unlovely, weak, despised – in short
Beset with sufferings of every sort.

In which this wretched man, as well as I,
Like a promontory
That faces north, and which a stormy sea
Pounds against incessantly,
Meets waves of suffering which he's pummelled by.

ANTIGONE: Here he comes! I *think* I recognise
    Our visitor. No one's with him, and his eyes –
    They overflow with tears.

OEDIPUS: So: who is he?

ANTIGONE: The very man we'd taken him to be
    From the first: Polyneices.

    Enter Polynices.

POLYNICES: Ah! Whose woes
    Shall I bewail first, sisters? Mine, or those
    I see before me – my old father's? Now
    An exile with you in a strange land, how
    Squalid his clothing is! It's clung for years
    To his decaying body, and appears
    To fester on his flesh like a disease –
    His unkempt hair blows wildly in the breeze.
    To match this, there's the food he's carrying
    To fill his wretched belly. Everything,
    Wretch that I am, I'm finding out too late.
    I've neglected you. A reprobate,
    That's what I am, and let me be the one
    To confess it. Yet Zeus shares his throne
    With Mercy. Let her stand at *your* side too,
    Father, for there have been grave faults, it's true –
    At any rate they can't be added to –
    Only amended. *(pause)* But you don't speak – why?
    Don't turn your back on me. Won't you reply?

    Pause.

    Will you insult me, then? Send me away
    In silence? And won't you even say
    What has enraged you? Make him say something,
    Sisters. He's obdurate. He's unyielding.
    Don't let him pack me off without my due –
    An answer – when the god is with me, too.

ANTIGONE: Tell him what you need. For words, be they

Pleasing, *dis*pleasing, pitiful, are a way
Of making people break their silence.

POLYNICES: Now,
That's sound advice. I'll tell him. *(to Oedipus)* Tell you how
I have been exiled... When I claimed the throne,
Being your elder son: the younger one –
Eteocles – wooed Thebes. Defeating me
Neither in combat nor contròversy,
He hounded me out of my native land
And into exile. Now I understand
What lies behind this – it must surely be
The curse on you and all your family –
Soothsayers also said as much to me –
In Argos, where I married the princess
And made the chiefs, men honoured for prowess
In battle, my allies. With this in view:
To raise a force, which they would help me do –
A sevenfold force to march on Thebes. I'll give
My life in this just cause of mine, or drive
Usurpers from the land. First let me say
That when I supplicate you I convey
My partners' prayers as well – the six great men
Already at the walls of Thebes. Well, then:
As I set out to make my brother pay
For stealing my realm from me, put away
Your anger, father – by your daughters here
And by your life, I beg of you. It's clear,
If any oracle was ever true,
Whichever side receives support from you
Is bound to be victorious. So my plea
Is that you let yourself be swayed by me –
By the gods of our house, yield. For we –
Yes, both of us – lead lives of beggary –
We survive by grovelling, in exile.
Our fate is just the same. At home, meanwhile,
The happy tyrant laughs at us. And oh,
How sad it makes me! If you help me, though,
I'll quickly send him packing, and put you
Back in your own house – put myself back too
In my place. Father, my proud boast can be

That I have done all this, if you agree
To take my part. But if you're not with me
I doubt if I'll return alive.

CHORUS: It *was*
Theseus who sent him to you, and because
He did, you mustn't send the boy *away*
Without first saying what you ought to say.

OEDIPUS: Very well, since Theseus sent him here –
Only because he did, with the idea
That I should speak to him, I shall do so.
Otherwise he would have had to go
Unanswered. Yes, and what he'll have to hear
Is hardly going to fill his life with cheer.
(to Polynices) Wretch! When you had the sceptre and the throne
That your brother has now made his own
You drove me out of Thebes – you exiled me,
Your father – made me citiless. To see
The rags I wear may make you weep, now *you*
Are in no less distress than I, but who,
If not you must be blamed for what I wear?
The time for tears is past. I have to bear
This load my whole life long, and think of you
As of a murderer, each day I do.
You filled my life with pain; you cast me out –
I beg for bread now, like a layabout,
From strangers – *you're* to blame. But I *have* got
Two daughters who have helped me. Had they not
I would be dead – I've had no help from *you*.
They nurse me and they keep me safe – these two.
They're men, not girls, as far as duty goes.
You boys – who are you? Hmm? Whose sons? Who knows?
Not mine. Fate's watching you, and soon – not yet –
Will punish you – that's if your force is set
On seizing Thebes. You'll never overthrow
That city. You, and Eteocles also,
Both bathed in blood, will fall in combat first.
I spoke those words (or some such) when I cursed
The pair of you before. Let that curse now
Fight for me – let it teach you both just how

Sons should treat fathers – giving them their due –
Respect, not scorn – the total scorn you two,
Because I'm blind, have shown me – something they –
My girls – have never done. And in this way –
By cursing – I completely nullify
Your supplication – make your coming by
The throne of Thebes impossible. That's so
If Justice, as revealed long years ago
To men, still sits with Zeus – if ancient laws
Hold good. Now go. Your father both abhors
And here disowns you. Go at once, I say!
Vilest of creatures! You can take away
These curses with you: you will lose the war,
Not seize your native land, and, furthermore,
Never return to Argos. You will die,
Killed by the brother you were exiled by,
Whom *you* will kill. That's how I curse you, so
Let your allies and the Thebans know
How Oedipus has favoured his two sons.

CHORUS: *(to Polynices)* You made two journeys – ill-considered ones –
           The first to Argos, and the second here.
           Now go – go quickly.

POLYNICES: Then I'm lost! It's clear
           That I should not have come. I'm full of fear
           For my poor comrades. What were we about
           (Disastrous enterprise!) when we set out
           From Argos? How that expedition ends
           I know, but cannot tell my new-found friends,
           Nor turn them back again. What can I do
           But meet this doom in silence? Sisters, you
           Have heard his cruel curse – if it all comes true –
           What he's called down on me – and if you then
           Manage to get back home to Thebes again,
           Give me a burial, I beg of you,
           With all the rites that are a dead man's due.
           Don't dishonour me. The praise you've won
           From Oedipus for all that you have done
           For *him* will be increased immeasurably
           By new praise, won for what you do for me.

ANTIGONE: Polynices, grant me this...

POLYNICES: Antigone –
Beloved sister – name it.

ANTIGONE: Turn your force
Back home to Argos – don't pursue a course
Leading to Thebes' destruction and to yours.

POLYNICES: How can I turn it back? Could I again,
Having once shown fear, ever lead those men?

ANTIGONE: Why should your anger reawaken, though?
Brother, what profit can you hope to show
From sacking Thebes – *your* city?

POLYNICES: What *disgrace*
A man who runs away from war must face –
A man whose younger brother mocks him.

ANTIGONE: Why,
Then what you heard our father prophesy
Will surely be: your death, and Eteocles'.

POLYNICES: Because he *wants* us dead. But prophesies
Can always be defied.

ANTIGONE: I'm wretched, then.
But who will follow you? Who'll dare to, when
They hear what he's foretold?

POLYNICES: I won't report
Bad tidings – news of an inspiring sort
Or none – that's what a leader tells his men.

ANTIGONE: You've made your mind up.

POLYNICES: Don't detain me, then.
I must now make this journey, though it's fraught
With danger and ill omen of the sort
He and his Furies threaten. As for you,

Antigone, Ismene – if you do
What I've requested of you when I'm gone
(I know that, for as long as I live on,
You can do *nothing* for me) may Zeus make
Both your lives happy. Goodbye. I must break
Away from you embrace. Never again
Are you to see me living.

ANTIGONE: All this pain.

POLYNICES: Don't mourn for me.

ANTIGONE: But I *must* mourn for you
Since I can see it – what you're running to –
Certain death.

POLYNICES: Well, if I'm doomed to die
I'll die.

ANTIGONE: No! Please! I'm pleading with you.

POLYNEICES: Why?
Your pleading is misplaced.

ANTIGONE: What misery!
Then I'm to lose you.

POLYNICES: Whether that will be
Lies in the lap of Chance. Meanwhile, I pray
That the gods keep all suffering away
From you and from Ismene. Everyone
Knows how much sorrow *you* deserve – that's none.

Exit Polynices. A peal of thunder off.

OEDIPUS: Who can we send?
Who will go and fetch my friend?

ANTIGONE: You want to see Theseus?

A second peal of thunder.

OEDIPUS: This thunder has been sent by Zeus
             And it's about to usher me away
             To Hades. *(to Chorus)* Have him brought here. Don't delay.

             More thunder.

CHORUS: He's here now.

             Enter Theseus.

OEDIPUS: Theseus, I'm about to die.
             It's time to keep my promise to you.

THESEUS: Why?
             What are the signs that tell you so?

OEDIPUS: These are –
             Thunder and lightning, sent by Zeus.

THESEUS: So far
             It's been as you've foretold. What must I do?

OEDIPUS: Son of Aegëus, I'll unfold to you
             A blessing for your city that will be
             For all time. Soon – with no one guiding me –
             I'll lead you to the place where I must die –
             A secret place. Tell no one where. Here's why:
             That way it will be *your* defence, and one
             That does what armies never could have done.
             These are mysteries, and it's not for me
             To speak of them, but you yourself shall see,
             Once there. I mustn't tell your people here.
             Or my daughters, though they are so dear.
             You must keep the secrets witnessed there
             And, when you die, disclose them to your heir –
             To him alone – he'll pass them on to his –
             And so on through time. Thus this city is,
             And will be, safe from any Theban threat.
             States may be governed sensibly, and yet
             Become aggressors. Yes, it's often so –
             And for some trivial cause. The gods are slow

But *sure* to punish people when they spurn
All shape or form of godliness, and turn
To acts of madness. You must not pursue
That course. But then I needn't preach to you –
What I'm saying – well, it's hardly new –
You know it all. The god is urging me
And we must go now to the place, quickly.
You must come with me, children. Strange to say,
I'm *your* guide now as *you* were mine. This way.
Don't touch me. Let me find, without your aid,
The tomb in which I'm destined to be laid –
My sacred tomb, in Attica. Straight ahead.
Come! *Quickly!* For the Goddess of the Dead
And Hermes lead me *this* way. Light! Oh, light!
No light to me today, though once as bright
To *me* as other men – this light I feel
For the last time. I go now to conceal
Myself in Hades' depths. But, dearest friend,
To you, your land, your subjects, may Heaven send
Good fortune. As you prosper, think of me –
The dead – and prosperous you will always be.

> *Oedipus goes, followed by Antigone, Ismene, Theseus*
> *and Attendants.*

CHORUS: If to honour you with prayers is right,
Great unseen goddess, and you, lord of the children of the night,
Aïdoneus, Aïdoneus, we pray
That the stranger may
Pass without any suffering, any pain,
Down to the Kingdom of the Dead below –
The fields through which the Styx's waters flow.
His grief and torment were as undeserved as they were great.
The gods are just, though, and will compensate
For all this by exalting him again.

Hear, Hades, you who keep your court down there,
Where Cerberus, as ancient legend tells us, has his lair
At the gates through which there crams an endless crowd,
And from his cave barks loud –
Hades' fierce watchdog. Son of Tartarus

And Earth – yes, Death – there's something you can do:
See that Cerberus lets the stranger through
Unscathed, without obstruction, as he passes on his way
Down to the land of the dead. For this we pray
To you, that send eternal sleep to us.

MESSENGER: King Oedipus has gone.

CHORUS: His wretchedness –
It was unequalled. Now it's over?

MESSENGER: Yes.
You may be sure he's passed from us.

CHORUS: But how?
Heaven took the man? He didn't suffer?

MESSENGER: Now,
It's something wonderful you've touched on there:
You've all been here a while, and you're aware
Of how he'd left this place – of how he'd shown
The rest of us the way, but all alone –
No friend to help him. At the gully known
As the Threshold, where steps of brass lead down
Right into earth's deep roots, he paused, in one
Of many branching paths, a brief walk on
From the particular hollow rock, in fact,
That's a memorial now, and marks the pact
Perithöus and Theseus made for good.
At equal distances from where he stood
There were the following: *(points to illustrate)* the Thorician stone -
The pear-tree known to all (the hollow one) –
The marble tomb. Loosening his squalid gown
He called his daughters to him and sat down.
They were to fetch him water from a spring
He said, so he could make an offering
And wash with it as well. Now, in full view
Was the hill sacred to Demeter, who
Protects the tender plants. There the girls went,
Returning soon with what they had been sent
To fetch for him. They washed him, dressed him, then

Zeus of the Dead sent thunder down, and when
They heard it, both girls shuddered. Then they wept,
Falling at their father's knees, and kept
Beating their breasts, and wailing loudly too.
Hearing their bitter cries, what could he do
But put his arms around the pair and say:
"Children, your father's life must end today."
I've nothing left to live for. You will be
Relieved now of your load. Yes, tending me
Was not a light one, children – that I know.
One word makes all your trouble nothing though:
Love. You had love from me, such as no one
Has ever given you. But from now on
You'll live your lives without me." So they cling
To one another, sobbing, sorrowing –
The father and his daughters – weep their fill
And then fall silent. Everything is still.
Then suddenly a voice cries: "Oedipus!"
A thunderous voice that frightens all of us.
Our hair stands right on end. Time and again
The god calls out to him: "You're coming, then?
Why do you keep me waiting, Oedipus?"
He knows that it's the god who calls him thus
And asks for Theseus to approach. The king
Obeys. Oedipus says: "My friend, one thing
You must please promise me: do not forsake
My daughters – give them your right hand and take
His, children. Make the pledge a solemn one.
Protect them, Theseus – see that all is done
To further their best interests: always do
Whatever seems most sensible to you,
Their firm – their only friend." The best of men,
Betraying not a trace of sorrow, then
Promised to do this – swore an oath, while he –
Oedipus – groping since he couldn't see,
Reached for his children. He had this to say:
"Children, the two of you must slip away.
Be brave. Your blood is royal. This is a sight
You mustn't see – and it would not be right
For you to hear what's said next. That being so,
Don't *ask* to see or hear, but simply go,

And quickly, too. Theseus alone will stay
And witness what occurs next, since he may –
It is his right." We heard and went away,
Following the girls – all weeping – sorrowing.
Quite soon, though, looking back, we saw the king –
No sign of Oedipus. There Theseus stood.
It seemed it was a sight that no one could
Endure to see, that he'd that moment seen.
He held his hands before his face to screen
His dazzled eyes. And then he said a prayer,
Saluting earth and heaven – heaven, where
The gods live. What took Oedipus away –
What obscure doom, Theseus alone can say.
It was no tempest rising from the sea,
Nor Zeus's thunderbolt. It seems to me
It must have been a messenger from heaven.
Or was the underworld – earth's firm base – riven
To let him enter – riven out of *love:*
He felt no pain – his passing was to prove
Free from all sickness, from all suffering,
All lamentation, and indeed a thing
Most wonderful – as wonderful, or more,
Than any mortal could have asked Heaven for.
All nonsense, you may think. You're welcome to.
Nor will I waste my time persuading you.
Call me a fool.

CHORUS: His daughters – where are they?

MESSENGER: They're coming now – they can't be far away.

Enter Antigone and Ismene.

ANTIGONE: Now, two wretched sisters, we are ready to deplore
            The curse our father handed down to us – as well we might:
            Why should we hold back? We bore
            Long, ceaseless hardship for him while he lived. We've seen a sight,
            Suffered a loss that baffles us.

CHORUS: Yes?
            What happened?

ANTIGONE: We can only guess.
                  But Oedipus passed on as you'd have wanted – didn't die
                  In battle, drown at sea –
                  The death that swept him off so suddenly
                  To Hades' depths was strange. We're *all* but dead now, she and I:
                  Where will we find our meagre livelihood, wandering away
                  To some far-distant land – sailing the seas.

ISMENE: I couldn't say.
                  I wish death-hungry Hades might join *me*
                  With my old father: What's our life now? Only misery.

ANTIGONE: Lost sorrows can be longed for, then! What nobody could bear
                  Was more than bearable while I could hold him. Father – oh,
                  Beloved father! – now you wear
                  The gloom of Hades like a garment. One
                  We never take off once we've put it on.
                  And we shall love you even there.

                  Forever he will lie
                  In darkness – in the grave,
                  Leaving us behind to wail and grieve.
                  For with these eyes, from which the tears stream, dearest father, I
                  Weep for your loss. Nor can I think of any way to quell
                  The sorrow and the grief that swell
                  Within me.

ISMENE: What new fate awaits us now?
                  We're orphans, sister.

CHORUS: But consider *how*
                  Your father died – his happy end – and then
                  Say to yourselves: "No more laments!", children.
                  We must all suffer.

ANTIGONE: Sister – let's hurry back there.

ISMENE: Why?

ANTIGONE: I want to see our father's tomb.

ISMENE: You still don't understand.

ANTIGONE: I've missed some point, have I?

ISMENE: And...

ANTIGONE: You've some objection?

ISMENE: Don't you know
He had to die alone – receive no burial.

ANTIGONE: So?
Just lead me to the place and then kill *me*.

ISMENE: I'm wretched, helpless; where am I to live? I've nobody.

CHORUS: Have courage, children.

ANTIGONE: Where am I to go?

CHORUS: You have a refuge.

ANTIGONE: Yes?

CHORUS: You're safe.

ANTIGONE: I think...

CHORUS: Well...?

ANTIGONE: I don't know
How we're to get home.

CHORUS: Why not stay?

ANTIGONE: Such suffering!

CHORUS: There was suffering yesterday.

ANTIGONE: Worse now. What comfort can there be
For us? What hope have we?

Enter Theseus.

THESEUS: Come, children, no more tears, Today
              When death was welcome – a relief –
              The gods' gift – there's no place for grief –
              To tempt their wrath is *not* the way.

ANTIGONE: Theseus, please – we beg of you...

THESEUS: A request?

ANTIGONE: We want to see
              Our father's tomb...

THESEUS: That cannot be.

ANTIGONE: Why not?

THESEUS: No one's permitted to.
              Your father told me not to go
              Near the place; tell nobody
              Where it was, enjoining me
              To keep faith with him. Doing so
              Would keep this *city* safe. I swore.
              Zeus – Horkos, too, who witnesses
              All oaths, have heard me swear.

ANTIGONE: This *is*
              His will. We'll be content, therefore.
              But send us home: we may prevent
              The shedding of our brother's blood.

THESEUS: Granted. If I can do you good
              In any way – and so content
              The friend we've just lost, it will be arranged.
              I shall spare no pains.

CHORUS: *(to Antigone and Ismene)* – No more tears, then.
              Never take up that mournful strain again.
              All this was pre-ordained and can't be changed.